The English Garden

HANS VON TROTHA is a German historian, novelist and journalist who spent ten years as editorial director of the Nicolai publishing house in Berlin. He is regarded as a specialist in the landscape gardens of the eighteenth century. Since then, he has worked independently as a curator, publicist, and consultant in the field of culture, including as a freelance journalist for *Deutschlandfunk Kultur*. In 2020–2021, he was curator of the Moosbrand Music and Literature Festival of the Nantesbuch Foundation. His books, *The English Garden* and *Pollak's Arm* have been translated into English.

JOHN BROWNJOHN (1929–2020) was a British literary translator. He translated more than 160 books and won the Schlegel-Tieck Prize for German translation three times and the Helen and Kurt Wolff Prize once. Brownjohn also collaborated with filmmaker Roman Polanski on *Tess* (1978), *Pirates* (1986), and *The Pianist* (2002) among others.

The English Garden

A Journey Through its History

Hans Von Trotha

Translated by John Brownjohn

First English edition published in 2009 by
HAUS PUBLISHING LTD
4 Cinnamon Row
London SW11 3TW

This first paperback edition published in 2024

A CIP catalogue record for this book is available from the British Library

ISBN: 978-1-914982-09-5

Designed and typeset in Garamond by MacGuru Ltd

Printed in the United Kingdom by Clays Ltd, Elcograf S.p.A.

Contents

The English Garden Tour

'I had long been acquainted with Nature's most sublime manifestations when I gazed ... into an English garden for the first time in my life,' the Swiss philosopher and physician Johann Georg Zimmermann wrote in 1785. He went on: 'I was still unacquainted with the art whereby wretched sand hills are transformed by a new kind of creation into an agreeable landscape... I still did not know that Nature can be represented in such charming diversity and noble simplicity within a very small area. I had yet to learn that one can, at first sight, be so carried away ... by Arcadian voluptuousness.... I still bless the day when I first discovered this.'

The English garden that sent Zimmermann into such transports of 'Arcadian voluptuousness' was not in England but at Marienwerder, near Hanover. 'English gardens' were coming into being all over Europe towards the end of the eighteenth century. Miniature landscapes that looked as if they had developed naturally, they were works of art imitative of Nature itself. They consisted of artificial lakes, manmade hills, imitation rocks and specially planted woods. The English author Horace Walpole hit the nail on the head when he wrote that the modern gardener displayed his talents by disguising his art.

One wonders why artists should have invested so much time and money, only to create the impression that they had done nothing at all. Besides, can Nature ever be imitated sufficiently well for us to mistake the copy for the original? The answer to that question seems a straightforward 'no', yet this is just what constitutes the charm of eighteenth-century English gardens. Well aware that they could never achieve their aim, landscape gardeners worked tirelessly to negate that realization. In so doing, they relied less on size than on the effect of their imitations of natural scenery. With great ingenuity, they endeavoured to stage their artificial landscapes as effectively as possible. Since the world could not be recreated on its original scale, they resorted to optical illusions and devices, ingenious allusions and surprise effects, so as to stimulate visitors to their gardens, to whet their imagination and – even when they were confronted by inappropriate copies – to evoke appropriate reactions.

The English garden at Wörlitz, near Dessau, even boasted a volcano that could be made to erupt as required. It was, of course, far smaller than Vesuvius, which it imitated. Mountains cannot be uprooted, but it was thought that even volcanoes and alpine peaks could be reproduced in such a way that one not only recognized their originals but was as moved and impressed as one would have been by the sight of the real thing. In order to acquaint visitors with the charm of foreign climes and bygone eras, artificial landscapes were provided with Greek temples, Gothic ruins, Palladian villas, hermitages, Chinese pavilions, pyramids, bridges, grottoes and triumphal arches. And visitors to such gardens went along with this. Far from laughing at these miniature replicas, they accepted them for what they were: invitations extended by copies of things to envision the things themselves. This was all the easier because most people had never seen these at first hand and were, at most, familiar with them from paintings, prints or travel books. Yet the imitation alps at Marienwerder were capable of dispelling 'the blackest melancholy and the most frightful homesickness', those being the emotions that afflicted Johann Georg Zimmermann, the Swiss visitor, during his first few weeks in Germany. 'I entered the little garden,' he enthused, '... and for the space of that day my homesickness was gone.'

The surviving artificial landscapes of the eighteenth century have lost none of their charm. Several English gardens of that period have survived in Germany, for instance at Wörlitz, in Weimar, in the Seifersdorfer Tal near Dresden, at Machern near Leipzig, at Schwetzingen, Schönbusch, Kassel-Wilhelmshöhe, Burgsteinfurt, Emkendorf, Munich and Potsdam. In its own way, and in areas of varying size, each of these parks endeavours to portray Nature in all its 'charming diversity', and each presents a series of surprises that transform an afternoon walk into a journey into another world. Although we may no longer be sent into transports of 'Arcadian voluptuousness' as readily as our eighteenth-century forebears, the fanciful creativity inherent in these gardens, together with the delight they take in playing with our imagination, their interest in alien religions and buried civilizations, and, last but not least, their elaborate attempts to realize the dream of an ideal landscape, continue to wield a very special charm – provided, of course, that we respond to their playful individuality.

Christian Cay Lorenz Hirschfeld, a professor of philosophy from Kiel, enlightened his fellow countrymen on the nature of the English garden in a five-volume *Theorie der Gartenkunst* [Theory of Garden Design], published at Leipzig between 1779 and 1785. According to Hirschfeld, its function was 'not merely entertainment of the outward sense, but true, inward uplifting of the soul, enrichment of the imagination and refinement of the emotions; ... ennoblement of the works of Nature and beautification of an earth that is, for a span, our home.' Seldom has any art been as highly esteemed as garden design in the eighteenth century.

Gardens have always been more than beautiful places in which to go for walks. The history of garden design is a history of attempts to recapture at least a modicum of our paradise lost, of the primeval garden from which humankind was expelled and of which every age seems to have a different conception. Every garden suggests how that paradise may have looked, and, at the same time, reflects the yearnings and wishful thinking of the age in which it has come into being. The word 'paradise', which is derived from an Old Persian dialect, originally signified an enclosed royal game preserve. Delimitation, or separation from the open countryside, is the defining characteristic of all gardens. This applied as much to the villa gardens of the ancient world as it does to those of the Italian Renaissance, the ancestors of all modern garden design.

Louis XIV made the seventeenth-century garden symbolize his conception of absolute monarchy. At Versailles his garden architect André Le Nôtre created an artistic synthesis of garden and palace which conveyed an unmistakable and universally perceptible idea of the king's view of the world and claim to authority. The only ideal view of the park – the overall view required by the strict symmetry to which its clipped trees, shrubs and hedges are also subject – was reserved for the king alone, because it was only when seen from the king's apartment on the first floor of the palace that the geometrical shapes on either side of the majestic central axis revealed their full splendour. The symmetry and beauty of Versailles is also a symmetry eloquent of power and centred on the Sun King himself; that was what Louis XIV wished to demonstrate to all who saw it. And everyone got the message. All over Europe, princes and big landowners emulated him by following the example of Versailles. From Drottningholm to Schönbrunn, French gardens sprang up everywhere: regular terraces and formal parterres with symmetrically arranged flower beds and borders in which trees, shrubs, and flowers disposed in geometrical patterns formed an open-air extension of the imposing palaces and mansions to which they belonged.

The situation in England was no different. In 1688, however, when the absolutist Stuart dynasty was deposed and English society underwent a fundamental change as a result of the so-called Glorious Revolution, a new era dawned. In joint allusion to ancient Rome's cultural heyday under Emperor Augustus and the second forename traditionally borne by their country's new kings from the house of Hanover, the English confidently christened it the 'Augustan Age'. It proved to be a golden age in which royal authority, rather than the liberty of the subject, was

Versailles
View of the park (c. 1670)

curtailed. The formal discipline of the French garden being incompatible with this new spirit of freedom, the Glorious Revolution was succeeded by a revival of garden design so fundamental that even contemporaries referred to it as revolutionary. At first sight, this revolution consisted in discarding all that gardens had hitherto done to delight the eye and, above all, to impress the beholder. What remained soon looked as if it were Nature itself, not art at all. Before long, noblemen throughout Europe had ceased to emulate the France of Louis XIV and were taking their cue from 'Augustan' England. English gardens – open landscapes in

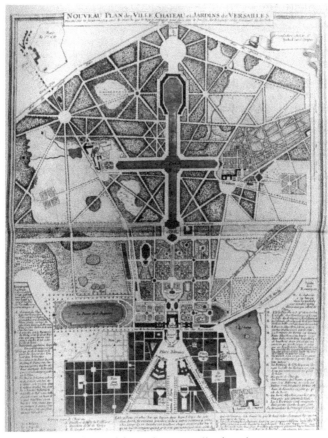

Plan of the park at Versailles (1714)

which free people could move around freely – were coming into being everywhere.

Political reorientation cannot, of course, engender a revolution in the history of art on its own. Although gardens may reflect social systems and claims to political authority,

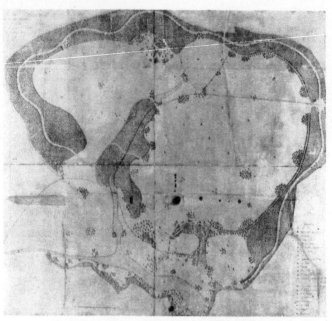

Plan of the garden of Bowood, Wiltshire (1763)

they are first and foremost works of art. They betray a great deal about a period's ideal of beauty, about aesthetic vogues, and people's relationship to Nature. Nowhere do art and Nature impinge on each other more directly than in a garden, the area between house and countryside in which people mould Nature to suit themselves.

During the Italian Renaissance and French Baroque, gardens were a part of the house. The architect laid down the rules according to which gardeners disposed of soil and plants. The open countryside was excluded by garden walls and box hedges. This did not change until the eighteenth century. In England, the motherland of the garden revolution, we can still trace how garden design was reinvented at this time, how formal French parks became so-called landscape gardens, and how garden architects became landscape gardeners. The consequences of the garden revolution become particularly apparent when plans of French and English gardens are examined side by side. The centralist symmetry of the formal Baroque garden is especially easy to reproduce on paper. The bird's-eye view on which such plans are based reveals the garden's message at a glance. We discern its meaning without further explanation. English gardens, on the other hand, require us to visit them in order to learn what they have to tell us. Much of what delighted eighteenth-century visitors to English gardens is still – or once more – surprisingly apparent to us today: a playful delight in simulation, an appeal to the power of imagination, and a constant striving for ever stronger effects. Our veneration for historic works of art often precludes us from drawing parallels and perceiving that, even in earlier times, there existed media intended simply to entertain the visitor and beholder.

But more was involved than that, of course. Writing in his own periodical *Der Genius der Zeit* [The Spirit of the Age], the popular philosopher August Hennings stated in 1797: 'It is quite possible ... that, while the political reformer strives vainly to bring about a revolution in people's way of thinking, the fine art of garden design will effect a complete reform in people's sentiments and ideas; and who can deny that such a reform would be the gentlest and most beneficial of all?' The new gardens reflected a new mode of thought and ensured its dissemination.

In the sixteenth century the villa gardens of the Italian Renaissance set the pattern for all European gardens. In the seventeenth century the French garden convincingly translated the spirit of the age into artistic forms. Europe's world view during the eighteenth century is inherent in the English gardens of the time. Their most striking feature was a new relationship between art and Nature. Eighteenth-century English gardens gave birth to the landscape ideal that governs our view of Nature to this day.

During the Renaissance and Baroque, beauty was ascribed to whatever conformed to abstract categories such as symmetry, proportion, numerical harmony and regularity. Nature could not provide all these, at least while trees were not planted in avenues and shrubs not pruned into geometrical shapes. Untamed, unpredictable Nature was regarded as hostile, misanthropic and dangerous. It was considered beautiful only when modified and adapted to the aesthetic conventions of the time. This applied not only to gardens but to the landscape painting whose first flowering occurred during the seventeenth century, mainly in Italy. The works of Claude Lorrain, which were regarded during the eighteenth century as the acme of landscape painting, do not show Nature as it is, but beautified, harmonized and idealized. If we contemplate and classify Nature according to aesthetic points of view, we call it landscape.

During the seventeenth century it was not yet customary to enjoy Nature itself as landscape. The aesthetic conquest of Nature did not occur until the eighteenth century. This process, too, will be explored during our journey through the history of the English garden. It culminated at a time

Claude Lorrain: Landscape with Jacob,
Laban and his daughters (1654)

when gardens were barely distinguishable from the surrounding landscape and people set out to view the open
countryside with garden-attuned eyes. It was the time in
which modern tourism has its roots.

August Wilhelm Schlegel once remarked, rather smugly,
that garden design was 'the only fine art' in which the
English could 'lay claim to originality'. This may explain
why England devotes more effort to preserving its historic
gardens than any other country in Europe. Nowhere else
was a greater area converted into gardens than in England
during the eighteenth and nineteenth centuries.

The following journey through the history of the
English garden confines itself to a few of the most beautiful, important and original of the landscape gardens of the
first generation still accessible to the modern visitor. Since

those gardens have always aspired to stimulate the senses and convey their messages as effectively and comprehensibly as possible, this journey will not be an excursion into the abstract heights of art history, but an outing filled with surprises and discoveries. Any readers or walkers who have familiarized themselves with the way in which these gardens imitate the world and entertain, instruct and impress the visitor will see all English gardens with different eyes, irrespective of what country they are in.

Touring the gardens of England is a traditional pastime. The 'English garden tour' has been an institution since the middle of the eighteenth century, when it became fashionable to travel from place to place, seeing and experiencing for oneself what the latest gardens had to offer. Travellers from the Continent studied them closely with a view to creating their own English gardens at home. Owners of gardens prepared for this invasion by providing suitable overnight accommodation in purpose-built lodging houses, and many of them made horse-drawn conveyances available for the use of visitors. In Goethe's novel *Die Wahlverwandtschaften* [Elective Affinities], which contains many references to garden design, an English peer on a visit to Germany complains: 'Who these days enjoys my buildings, my grounds, my gardens? Not I, nor even my family: foreign visitors; inquisitive, restless travellers.'

Travel also played an important part in the genesis of the English garden, and it always remained one of its underlying themes. The English custom of sending young gentlemen off on foreign tours before they took up office went back to Elizabethan times. It was intended that the youthful aristocrats should acquire some social polish and sophistication, gain experience (not least of a sexual nature), and complete their education. At first, the fact that the so-called Grand Tour took them to Italy was dictated primarily by political considerations. The region between the Alps and Rome enabled them to compare a greater diversity of systems of government than anywhere else in Europe. By degrees, however, their focus of interest shifted. In Italy, English participants in the Grand Tour not only became acquainted with an unfamiliar, sun-drenched landscape but came into contact with the vestiges of a bygone civilization: the architecture of classical antiquity. They brought back vast numbers of paintings, prints, drawings, books and antiques. Dozens of Italian landscape paintings came to England, where they disseminated an idealized image of Nature coupled with an enthusiasm for the culture of the ancient world. When the English finally developed a desire for some alternative to set against the rigidly formal garden designs of France, their noblemen's heads were filled with memories of the Italian landscape, both painted and idealized in retrospect, and of the buildings of Roman antiquity. Such were the exemplars on which they based their own version of paradise.

The new gardens fulfilled dreams and assuaged longings, not only in those who had visited Italy, but in all who had never had the opportunity to experience the landscape and culture of the Mediterranean at first hand. The English garden tour became a kind of substitute for the long journey across Europe, a Grand Tour in miniature that enabled one to become acquainted with the beauties of that world within a very small compass. August Hennings wrote in 1797: 'Just as art lovers formerly visited Rome and Florence in order to venerate masterworks of antiquity and of more recent times in the shape of statues and paintings; just as writers and travellers climbed the Volcano [Vesuvius] or Etna so as to be able to say that they had looked into the crater, and that the sun had risen from the sea before them; just as they travelled the glaciers to seek the source of the Rhine in eternal ice and pluck the children of spring on the borders of winter; just as [James] Bruce journeyed as far as Ethiopia in order to discover that the source of the Nile was a spring; and just as travellers in general have described churches, castles, palaces, balls, firework displays, comedies, military parades, parliamentary debates, harbours, gaming parties, posthouses and inns; so famous gardens are now being visited and described so accurately that one has only to read [such accounts] to convince oneself that the author was in a labyrinth of beauties in which one can go astray.'

Henry Flitcroft:
front elevation of Chiswick House (1727)

Palladian Revival, or the germ cell

Chiswick House, London

At the beginning of the garden revolution – and the historic English garden tour – stands a building. Garden design had, after all, been the business of the architect ever since the master builders of the Italian Renaissance revived the architecture of antiquity in tandem with the culture of the villa garden.

On the banks of the Thames, for example in the then small villages of Twickenham and Chiswick, the early years of the eighteenth century witnessed the development of a country house culture that formed a northern counterpart of the *villeggiatura* of the Italian Renaissance. This deliberate approximation to its Mediterranean exemplar is probably what first strikes a visitor to Chiswick House, the country seat of Richard Boyle, 3rd Earl of Burlington. Lord Burlington was one of the leading architects of his day. The country house he designed and built at Chiswick between 1720 and 1730 broke with all existing conventions. Many people seeing it for the first time are surprised, many amused as well. The white building is surmounted by a dome, and the portico rests on six Corinthian columns. Two handsome flights of steps adorned with vases complete its resemblance to an Italian Renaissance villa, and eight tall chimneys reminiscent of obelisks constitute another

Lord Burlington: drawing for the chimneys
at Chiswick House (before 1730)

striking feature. Although the forecourt of Chiswick House
seems to resonate with the noble simplicity and quiet grandeur of the ancients, which Renaissance architects had
revived, it fails to convince. This is not only because one
would expect to find such buildings in the sunlit Veneto
rather than a London suburb, but because they generally
date from the sixteenth century, not the eighteenth. What
mainly surprises one about Chiswick House is its proportions, which are all wrong. The dome is far too big relative to the rest of the building, the height of the chimneys
lends them a rather grotesque appearance, and, last but not
least, the whole house is far too small.

'Too small to live in, but too big to hang on one's watch-
chain,' was Lord John Hervey's verdict on seeing Chiswick
House. It should, perhaps, be pointed out that Hervey was
one of Burlington's fiercest political opponents. Above all,
though, one should bear in mind what Burlington meant
his villa to achieve. He was concerned not only to design a

country seat that was good to live in, but to set an example that would be visible from afar. Like a painting, his house was intended to create a mood and stimulate the imagination. That effect was more important to him than the laws of proportion. Lord Burlington's villa initiated a new fashion in English country house architecture, and numerous excursionists made pilgrimages to Chiswick to see it for themselves. Provided the Burlingtons were at home, Chiswick House was open to visitors in the afternoons. Similar provisions applied to most country houses of the time.

The architect of Chiswick House was born Richard Boyle in 1695 and died the 3rd Earl of Burlington in 1753, having inherited the title and estates in 1704, at the age of ten. Despite personal links with the Stuart kings in exile, Burlington established contact with the Whigs, the new political masters whose opposition to the royal house had brought about the Glorious Revolution of 1688, and who claimed to have introduced constitutional monarchy. After George II ascended the throne in 1727, Burlington remained close to the seat of power until May 1732, when he resigned from all his offices after clashing with Robert Walpole, the all-powerful Chancellor of the Exchequer. In company with his wife, his three daughters and the most important of his extensive collection of pictures, Burlington left his house in Piccadilly (which now houses the Royal Academy of Arts) and moved to Chiswick. Thanks to him, the little village became a cultural centre. He took in George Frederick Handel after the latter fell out with the royal court and patronized philosophers, writers, painters and, of course, architects. Horace Walpole christened him an 'Apollo of the arts' and Alexander Pope called him a latter-day Vitruvius.

Lord Burlington was an avowed opponent, not only of political absolutism, but of classicistic French architecture, and he found an alternative to it in Italy. The observant eye will note that he advertised his sources on the façade of Chiswick House, on which two statues identify the building's godfathers and the style it was to initiate: Andrea Palladio and Inigo Jones. Having made an exhaustive study of the architecture of the ancient world, read Vitruvius and surveyed ancient Roman buildings, Andrea Palladio (1508–80) had used this knowledge to mould the architecture of the High Renaissance into a distinct and consistent style. He was the author of those famous villas, mainly in the Veneto, which are sustained by the rhythm of their columns and pilasters and wholly dependent on their perfect formal harmony. The architect Inigo Jones (1573–1652) had introduced Palladian ideas into England at the beginning of the seventeenth century, but his initiative did not produce much in the way of results. It remained for Lord Burlington to effect a stylistic breakthrough and signal a Palladian revival. He could not have known that this would also signal a revival of European garden design.

Chiswick House was modelled on Palladio's Villa Rotonda in Vicenza (1550/1). Burlington was not, however, interested in producing a faithful replica of the original. He did not simply copy Palladio's villa, just as Palladio himself had not simply copied buildings of the ancient world. Instead, both men strove to apprehend the spirit of their historical exemplars and combine it with the requirements and ideals of their own day. They lent architecture fresh momentum by translating old designs into a contemporary mode, their underlying motive being a desire to hark back to the advanced civilization of the ancient world in order to present their contemporaries with a better alternative.

The Villa Rotonda's dome was designed according to the laws governing Italian Renaissance architecture, which were based on the classical theory of proportion and numerical harmony. Thus, in an ideal view of the front façade, the dome and the body of the building form a well-proportioned whole. To anyone standing immediately in front of the building, however, the dome is scarcely visible. Burlington, for his part, wanted his reproduction of the villa to look, even from the forecourt, like the original design. To achieve this, he reduced the portico in size and enlarged the dome, deliberately disrupting the laws of proportion in order to create a well-proportioned effect. Instead of recreating Palladio's building in England, he wanted to show everyone the impression he had formed of it. Chiswick House is more a reminiscence than a copy; it stands for an idea rather than for itself. The same applies to the size of the building; what matters is the image it presents, its picturesque effect, not its dimensions. Besides, Burlington needed no more room. The villa was only an annexe, not a house in its own right (the old country house has since been demolished).

In 1714, as befitted a young man of his rank, the brilliant and extremely wealthy Lord Burlington set off on a Grand Tour to Italy. He returned home in 1715 with hundreds of crates filled with paintings, drawings and books. Before

William Kent: Preliminary study for the hall of Chiswick House
(engraving by P. Fourdrinier, 1727)

long, in the summer of 1719, he paid another visit to Italy. His second Italian tour was devoted entirely to studying Palladio. This time he returned home not only resolved to build a Palladian villa of his own, but accompanied by some of Palladio's drawings and a young and unknown artist who was to assist him in his project: William Kent (1684–1748), who had been in Rome since 1709. Kent had made ends meet as a scene and coach painter until some noblemen recognized his talent and sent him off to Italy to continue his training. He provided Chiswick House with furniture and painted ceilings. More importantly, however, he advised Burlington on the design of a garden that would suit the building. The 'Apollo of the arts' had found his priest, as Horace Walpole remarked.

The villa was probably completed in 1729. Discounting its relative proportions, the design conformed in principle to the rules Palladio had formulated for the construction of villas. The excessively lofty dome looks even more disproportionate from inside, the hall it surmounts being too narrow and far too high. That was the price the architect paid for being less concerned about the proportions of the interior spaces than about the effect the building created from outside. A suite of three rooms leads off the hall in the north. These occupy the place Palladio had reserved for the loggia, an airy gallery, but one which, at Chiswick, had to be glazed to cope with adverse weather conditions. The decorative leafwork on the Corinthian columns connects the gallery with the garden, which can be seen through its windows.

In 1727, with Kent's assistance, Burlington began to

modify the garden to accord with the villa. (The poet Alexander Pope had advised him on its previous redesign around 1715.) His initial intention was to surround his 'new old' villa with the kind of garden that might have existed in the ancient world. This was consistent of him. Renaissance buildings were always associated with the spirit of antiquity, that vanished civilization whose artistic zenith was as legendary as its political achievements. It stood for the concept of democracy and resistance to tyranny, and its highly developed garden design was known from literary sources. Burlington supported attempts to reconstruct such gardens (Pliny's, for example) on the basis of surviving descriptions.

On the garden side, the villa at Chiswick adjoined a small grove of evenly spaced trees into which Burlington cut clearings and lines of sight. In place of the overall visibility characteristic of French gardens, he juxtaposed a diversity of garden spaces. Although this arrangement had little to do with the gardens of antiquity, it generated a mood that conformed to contemporary notions of antiquity with the aid of columns and sculptures (some of which Burlington had brought back from the Grand Tour), as well as small buildings reminiscent of classical temples and arches. In 1728, as an eye-catcher, Burlington cut a semicircular clearing out of the wood (the so-called EXEDRA), in which were displayed statues of Socrates, Lycurgus and Lucius Verus, three celebrated opponents of tyranny. This was probably a reference not only to Louis XIV, but also to Robert Walpole, who made men like Burlington feel cheated out of the political functions due to them by amassing more

Orange grove and Pantheon
(engraving of a painting by Pieter Andreas Rysbrack, c. 1729)

and more power until his resignation in 1742. We encounter this theme repeatedly in the landscape gardens of the first generation. Their allusion to the ancient world was not enough on its own, but always possessed contemporary relevance. No distinction was drawn in this respect between Greek originals, Roman copies and adaptations of the Italian Renaissance. What mattered was what was common to them all, at least in the eyes of English Grand Tourists: a cultural zenith and a model of society founded on liberty and self-determination.

It was this idea that promoted the dissemination of classical temples in the gardens. The three statues in the EXEDRA had originally been in one such garden temple, which Burlington erected in a small orange grove. It is the loveliest and most atmospheric place in Chiswick: a secluded, almost intimate garden area. After the manner of Roman amphitheatres, it is enclosed by grassy terraces on which stand orange trees in terracotta pots. They surround a pool with an obelisk jutting from it. The circular brick temple on the west side of the amphitheatre, which has a projecting portico, reminds one of the Pantheon in Rome. Too small to disrupt the prevailing atmosphere, it presents an allusive appearance sufficient to summon up the spirit of ancient Rome. And that was what inspired the building of the villa at Chiswick and the design of its garden.

As time went by, Burlington's artistic adviser William Kent clearly grew dissatisfied with the references to antiquity inherent in symmetrical garden areas. The contrived discipline of formal garden design was at odds with the spirit of freedom the classical buildings and sculptures were intended to convey.

Kent proceeded to eliminate any pools of geometrical design, allowed the trees to grow as they would, and endeavoured to lend the garden scenery an increasingly natural appearance. He was particularly successful when it came to the lake west of the house. This gently curving stretch of water, whose uneven, irregular banks were deliberately left unstraightened, resembles a river. Burlington christened it the BRENTA, after the river in the Veneto beside which Palladio had built some of his loveliest villas. This combination of architecture and garden created the image of an accessible landscape which reminded Burlington, Kent and other Grand Tourists of delightful scenes in the Campagna or the Veneto; it also gave those who had not visited Italy at least some inkling of their charm. Alexander

Pieter Andreas Rysbrack:
Garden scene at Chiswick (c. 1728)

Pope enthusiastically assured a correspondent that, to him, Chiswick was the loveliest place on which the sun had ever shone.

Kent transformed the lake's inflow into a cascade whose ruinous and pristine appearance was meant to emphasize the natural character of the scene. The best vantage point from which to view this factitiously natural-looking landscape is the so-called CLASSICAL BRIDGE, which did not acquire its classicistic shape until after Burlington's death. For work at Chiswick continued. His heirs and descendants pressed on with the naturalization of the villa garden until well into the nineteenth century. What has survived is the harmonious juxtaposition of the formal and the irregular, the germ cell of the eighteenth-century garden revolution. William Kent was the first to lend garden art a natural appearance so as to create atmospheric images. And, like all revolutionaries, he was soon criticized by his successors, who had progressed still further. Horace Walpole called him the father of modern garden design, but he also remarked: 'Having routed *professed* art, for the modern gardener exerts his talents to conceal his art, Kent, like other reformers, knew not how to stop at the just limits.'

Francis Jukes:
Strawberry Hill, Twickenham (1781)

Gothic Revival, or the house of the book
Strawberry Hill, Twickenham

Horace Walpole, Earl of Orford, was the epitome of what people of the eighteenth century called 'witty': a brilliant, quick-witted, cultivated eccentric who, rather than following fashions, initiated them himself. His father was none other than Sir Robert Walpole, the all-powerful chancellor who led the Whigs and, with the support of the first two Georges to occupy the British throne, who trusted him, dominated the politics of Great Britain for twenty years. Having been educated at Eton and Cambridge, as befitted his social status, Horace was sent off on the Grand Tour. He returned home in 1741. Being intended to follow in his father's outsize footsteps, he dutifully entered Parliament but remained an aesthete, thinker, art lover and writer to the end of his days.

When looking around for a country house in 1747, Walpole settled on Twickenham. Lord Burlington's friend Alexander Pope had died three years earlier, and his house at Twickenham, in whose garden Pope had experimented with natural shapes, had long been a popular attraction (although hardly any of it survives today apart from a pub by the name of *Pope's Grotto*). Walpole promptly embarked on his garden's redesign.

Although Horace Walpole's Strawberry Hill came into

being several decades after Burlington's Chiswick House and little of its garden has survived, a visit to Twickenham is well worthwhile. Here, too, it was mainly architecture that influenced the art of landscape gardening.

Despite his admiration for Lord Burlington, Walpole disliked Chiswick's noble, antique character. At Strawberry Hill he devised an alternative. Quoting from the Bible in a letter dated 1749, he wrote: 'When thou buildest a new house, then thou shalt make a battlement for thy roof, that thou bring not blood upon thine house, if any man fall from thence.' He was clearly thinking of the medieval castles and fortresses in which England abounded.

In 1751 Walpole decided 'to go Gothic', as he announced in another letter. He wanted to establish a link with the dark ages of his forefathers, not the ancient world; with the unexplored epoch intermediate between the advanced civilization of the ancients and the achievements of the present, which was wreathed in the mists of the unknown and the nimbus of the dark, eerie and primitive. But people had recently developed a taste for what they conceived of as untamed natural scenery, for the open countryside with its dark woods and rugged cliffs. They even constructed mountains, rocky caves and gloomy forest grottoes. Since garden designers could model their landscape scenery on all manner of natural features, why shouldn't people also take pleasure in a form of architecture that aroused feelings similar to those evoked by a waterfall in a damp grotto or a shadowy crag in a park? Walpole's response to the 'Palladian Revival' and the concomitant 'Greek Revival' was a 'Gothic Revival'.

Like Chiswick House, Strawberry Hill marked the beginning of a fashion that exerted a lasting effect on the history of architecture. At first, however, both styles flourished in the landscape gardens they not only enlivened but invested with meaning and deeper significance. Classical and classicistic temples, gateways and columns were symbolic of beauty, truth and goodness, of political grandeur, and of the wisdom and perfection that had once been achieved and had then been lost. Gothic, on the other hand, became a symbol of freedom and attachment to Nature. It was a reminder of a far-off time when Britons cultivated their island with self-confident self-determination.

Furthermore, Gothic pointed arches and ribbed vaults reminded people of precisely what they had learnt to appreciate in Nature: the rugged and lofty, the dark and irregular – all those characteristics that did not subordinate themselves to the classical laws of proportion. In Gothic buildings, pristine Nature seemed to come alive once more as an artistic form. Many people supposed Gothic to have originated in distant parts of the world such as India, Arabia, or the land of the Saracens. This stimulated their imagination. Having yet to discover that the arches, buttresses and clustered columns were born of static necessity, they mistook them for pure ornaments and a successful attempt to imitate natural effects; in other words, for precisely what the new English gardens were refining into an artistic system. They credited Old Gothic architecture with the picturesque, illusory character which neo-Gothic buildings possessed. Jane Austen is said to have seriously believed that English monasteries had been razed purely for the sake of picturesque effect.

Although Horace Walpole did not invent the Gothic revival, he did more than anyone else to promote its popularity. At Strawberry Hill he spent decades working himself into the world of Gothic. In the spring of 1750, together with John Chute and the painter Richard Bentley, nicknamed 'the Goth', he founded the Committee of Taste, whose task consisted in 'gothicizing' Strawberry Hill. None of trio was an architect, but Strawberry Hill is less a milestone in the history of architecture than testimony to the playful literary spirit that flourished in the landscape gardens of the eighteenth century and sometimes produced strange blooms. A plaque on the façade of Strawberry Hill proclaims: 'Horace Walpole. 1717–1797. Man of Letters. Lived here.' But Horace Walpole not only lived at Strawberry Hill; the house became the dominant focus of his life.

The narrow, uninviting entrance to the house is situated beyond a crenellated wall on the sunless north side. The hall is dark and rather creepy. In Walpole's day the only form of illumination in this area was a coloured glass lantern whose flickering light danced across grey stone walls. The gloom made it impossible to tell that they had been wallpapered, and that the 'stone' was merely a thick layer of paint. Even when visitors were aware of this, it made no difference to the shiver that ran down their spine. Although they naturally knew where they were, they could, if they wished, feel just as new arrivals in a medieval castle must have felt. And that was the whole point of the *mise en scène*.

Walpole called himself an architect with paste and scissors. He designed wallpapers that simulated spatial depth and made new walls look centuries old. His massive fireplaces were reminiscent of times gone by; their effect was not spoilt by the fact that they were constructed of wood and could never be used. Walpole's castle contains an oratory, a cloister, a refectory, and a gallery with a splendid vaulted ceiling of medieval appearance. Each room is a new experience, and the whole building is a mishmash of quotations and allusions, copies and clichés. Above all, though, it is a fantastic interplay of moods and effects. The fireplace in the Great Drawing Room is a reproduction of the tomb of Edward the Confessor in Westminster Abbey, the ceiling design modeled on the rose window in Old St Paul's, the roof of the library adorned with lines of Old Gothic script. In another room we suddenly find ourselves in the choir of Rouen Cathedral. Anything that whetted Walpole's Gothic imagination he transformed with the aid of saw and paintbrush into architectural features with which to improve his castle. Every detail tells its own story – or a story which Walpole, the man of letters, told about it. Appropriately enough, his world of deception and illusion included an art collection containing over forty copies but only three originals.

Walpole's Gothic aspirations were not, of course, confined to the interior decoration of his house but embraced its external conformation and surroundings. Even the cows in his grounds were selected for their colouring. He was particularly pleased with the so-called BEAUCLERC TOWER, built in 1776 and modeled on Thornbury Castle in Gloucestershire. 'I have carried this little tower higher than the round one,' he wrote, 'and it has an exceedingly pretty effect, breaking the long line of the house picturesquely, and looking very ancient.'

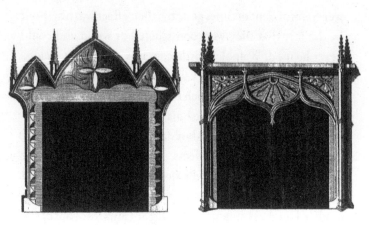

Richard Bentley:
Fireplace designs for Strawberry Hill

Little by little, Walpole began to live not only in this house but also in the world from which it quoted (not that this ever prevented him from making jokes about the miniature copies of which his 'cheesecake house' consisted). He was fond of dressing up to suit his surroundings. 'Tread softly,' he warned visitors, 'for you tread on my dreams.' During the night of 4–5 June 1764, he actually had a dream in which the stories from which he derived his inspiration acquired a life of their own. The staircase at Strawberry Hill, which had always been especially dear to his heart, played a prominent part in it. This dream became the novel of the house, a story in which medieval characters underwent all manner of wondrous experiences, and in which Walpole was able to give free rein to his exuberant imagination. *The Castle of Otranto. A Story* was first published at Christmas 1764. Some months later Walpole wrote to a

Edward Edwards:
Strawberry Hill, Treppenhaus (1784)

friend: 'Shall I even confess to you what was the origin of this romance? I waked one morning in the beginning of last June from a dream, of which all I could recover was, that I had thought myself in an ancient castle (a very natural dream for a head filled like mine with Gothic story) and

John Carter:
Strawberry Hill, the Holbein Room (1788)

that on the upper-most bannister of a great staircase I saw a gigantic hand in armour.... You will laugh at my earnestness, but if I have amused you by retracing with any fidelity the manners of ancient days, I am content, and give you leave to think me as idle as you please.'

Quite a few people considered Horace Walpole's activities at Strawberry Hill childish and futile. But his Gothic dreams derive their vitality from a play with something serious. Like the adventures of the medieval characters in his novel, the dummy fireplaces and doors in his house are facets of a grand illusion. Faith in that illusion and a determination to surrender to it are characteristic of Strawberry Hill, which is, above all, a game played with moods and emotions, utopias and possibilities. Many were genuinely enthralled by Walpole's game. They visited his castle and read his novel, of which twenty editions had appeared by 1800. He became a model for a whole generation of young writers, and hundreds of 'Gothic' thrillers were published, not only in England but on the Continent.

It was only natural that the success of Walpole's literary feat of the imagination should have encouraged him to press on with his most important project. He continued to add to Strawberry Hill after 1765, gradually transforming his castle beside the Thames into the place of which his novel had told. The Gothic revival at Strawberry Hill retained its dynamism even after his death, and building in the Gothic style had gained wide acceptance by the middle of the nineteenth century, outside gardens as well. At that time Walpole's castle passed into the possession of Lady Frances Waldegrave, who boldly went on adding to it. Ultimately, therefore, the house fell victim to the style it had initiated. In its present form, only the nucleus of Strawberry Hill rates as the oldest neo-Gothic house in Europe. It is probably also the only neo-Gothic building to have been 're-gothicized' at a later date.

William Kent:
The landscape at Rousham, complete with
Gothic eye-catcher (c. 1740)

Rousham House, Oxfordshire

C hiswick House and Strawberry Hill enable us to see, directly adjoining one another, the basic architectural shapes that brought the emerging landscape gardens to completion. The link between them was always Nature, which was, admittedly, quite as artificial as classicistic temples or Gothic walls. People were familiar with this combination of ancient buildings and idealized natural scenery from landscape paintings. The works of Jacob van Ruisdael, Poussin, Claude Lorrain and Salvator Rosa (who had specialized in rugged natural scenery) formed the basis of many important collections and served as models for the imitation of Nature in gardens.

Greek temples and Gothic ruins, miniature pantheons and medieval pavilions sprouted mushroomlike from the ground, which had formerly been ploughed and remodelled to accord with the compositional rules of landscape painting. These buildings were seldom as big as Chiswick House or Strawberry Hill (which were themselves smaller than the originals they strove to emulate). As a rule, this architecture in historical guise was adapted, not only in its effects but also in its dimensions, to the artificial landscapes in which it was set. Nature could not be successfully imitated without some manipulation of perception. Landscape gardeners depended on allusions being enough to steer the beholder's imagination in the requisite direction. That applied as much to Nature in a garden as it did to buildings. One milestone in the history of this exciting game with perception is the garden William Kent created at Rousham from 1738 onwards.

'Kentissime!' Horace Walpole exclaimed on entering that secluded little paradise amid the rolling hills of Oxfordshire. This was where, after his previous work at Chiswick, Kent was able to show how he envisioned an ideal landscape imbued with the spirit of antiquity. In 1738 he was commissioned by the brothers General James and Colonel Robert Dormer to redesign Rousham in contemporary style. Kent began by altering the house itself. He added some low side wings and designed the stables. The niches and quoins in the new façades create a rather odd impression, being at once a trifle Gothic and a trifle classical. Kent was inspired by both styles, and a rare but harmonious juxtaposition of both can be seen on the east side of the gardens, where Kent placed a GOTHIC SEAT in front of a PALLADIAN DOORWAY. In English gardens, Gothic and classical buildings are generally to be found separate and in landscape settings suited to their respective characters. (As a rule, landscape gardeners adhered to the conventions of landscape painting by favouring rocks and dark conifers for Gothic and paler, broadleaved trees for classical.) For Kent, however, a Grand Tourist and lover of Italy, the classical always predominated.

Beyond the house we come first to a big stretch of lawn,

the so-called *Bowling Green,* which was originally laid in 1720. Although Kent left this almost untouched, he lent it new significance. From there, with the house at our back, we seem to be looking out at a landscape painting: the grass slopes down to a river beyond which stretches a big, open meadow enclosed by trees. About a mile from the house, to emphasize the painterly effect still further and create an eye-catcher, Kent placed a triple archway in Gothic guise. On the edge of the *Bowling Green* he also erected a copy of a group sculpture from Tivoli representing a horse in combat with a lion. Thus, by the simplest means, he transformed the world for the beholder's benefit. Any yearnings for the promised land of the Grand Tourist are assuaged, at least illusorily: no longer standing on English soil and admiring a picture by an Italian landcape painter, visitors to the gardens suddenly find themselves back on a terrace in Tivoli, gazing out at an ideal picture of indigenous Nature with picturesque, ruined Gothic walls. At Rousham, this *mise en scène* initiates a Grand Tour in miniature.

Two sculpted heads invite us to enter the wood that borders the *Bowling Green* on either side. If visitors take the hint, they are introduced by degrees to an artificial world which Walpole called 'as elegant and antique as if the emperor Julian had selected the most pleasing seclusion about Daphne to enjoy a philosophical retirement.' This is where Kent moulded his image of Arcadia into a reality. The wood is threaded with narrow, winding paths. Under Kent, paths became one of the garden designer's most important means of artificially creating a natural impression and welding separate areas of garden scenery together. With the aid of carefully calculated bends and ingeniously planted trees and shrubs that allow of certain views only, the landscape gardener controls what the walker can see and when he sees it. Kent, who had ascertained that 'Nature abhors the straight line', designed garden paths that are never straight and always concealed from view by the next bend.

These 'serpentine walks' were soon threading their way through all English gardens. Of natural appearance, they always prevented the expectant walker from seeing what awaited him beyond the next bend. This generated suspense and enhanced the effect of individual areas of garden scenery. Winding paths render it quite possible to take the visitor on a labyrinthine journey in the course of which he quickly loses his sense of direction and gains the impression that a garden is of boundless extent. And boundlessness – Kent had observed that too – is one of the most important characteristics of Nature as opposed to art. Thus, anyone desirous of lending his garden a natural appearance was dependent on concealing its boundaries. Winding paths preclude an overall view. Forever uncertain what awaits them, visitors roam through a potentially endless series of landscape scenes of different character. Old General Dormer had given his gardener, John MacClary, precise instructions on how to show visitors around his garden. That would really have been quite unnecessary. In the landscape garden, the combination of paths and planting fulfill the function of a guide.

Kent's serpentine begins by leading us past the GOTHIC SEAT and PALLADIAN DOORWAY to a terrace. This presents us with another fine view of the surrounding countryside and transports us once more to Italy through the medium of a copy of a sculpture. The terrace is known as the Praeneste, after the ancient terraced town of Palestrina (Praeneste) not far from Rome. It was customary to name temples, scenes and buildings after their originals so as to assist the visitor's leap of the imagination. Only an interplay between landscape, garden architecture and vision could summon up the Arcadian worlds of the English garden. This process was assisted by rivers named the Styx, forest clearings known as Elysium, and so-called temples of Bacchus or grottoes of Venus.

Beyond the PRAENESTE TERRACE the path loses itself in the wood once more. As we approach the banks of an octagonal pool, the trees gradually reveal a cascade grotto bordered by statues on the edge of a clearing. Satyrs peer at us from the trees, and enthroned above the cascade is Venus, patroness of the grotto and the surrounding valley. The VENUS VALE, too, possesses an Italian exemplar: the grounds of the Villa Aldobrandini near Frascati.

The route now climbs a little. In its midst is a small, winding stream, a meandering rill that enlivens the natural bends of the serpentine walk. At the highest point of this part of the grounds Kent erected an idyllic little temple in the classical style. It is dedicated to the nymph Echo. An open book carved in stone reposes on an altar. From a bench in the temple one can gaze over the said book at the landscape beyond.

An Apollo on the edge of the wood points the way down to the river Cherwell, which borders the estate, a natural boundary, but one that is not perceived as such at all. Even where Nature has not provided such a boundary, however, no walls and fences are permitted to disrupt the illusion of the artificial landscape. Yet walls were needed, for instance to keep desirable animals inside a garden and undesirable ones out. This problem was solved by a device whose first use is considered to mark the birth of the landscape garden proper. Horace Walpole described it as follows: 'But the capital stroke, the leading step to all that has followed, was ... the destruction of walls for boundaries, and the invention of fosses – an attempt then deemed so astonishing, that the common people called them Ha! Ha's! to express their surprise at finding a sudden and unperceived check to their walk.'

The solution was both simple and ingenious: walls were sunk – erected below ground level – so as to be visible only when one was right on top of them. The ha-ha (the word has survived as a technical term) facilitates an unobstructed view where required and conceals the fact that a garden is finite. It effaces the boundary between art and Nature. As the visitor perceives it, and irrespective of its actual extent, the garden seems to vault the ha-ha and go on ad infinitum.

It is an ironical feature of the history of gardens that the first mention of the ha-ha occurs in, of all places, a work by a French author, Antoine-Joseph Dézallier d'Argenville's *La Théorie et la pratique du jardinage* of 1709. This book was translated into English in 1712, and there was already said to be a ha-ha at Blenheim in that year. By the 1730s at the latest, the ha-ha had become a staple feature of all new gardens. Wherever the river does not fulfil the function of a natural ha-ha, the grounds of Rousham, too, are separated from their surroundings by that invisible means.

The route follows the river Cherwell for a while. Then, quite suddenly, the trees part to reveal a view of the house. This comes as a surprise, because the undulations and meanderings of the garden path have caused us to lose our bearings. Thereafter, Kent impressively demonstrates that he was a master of garden design, and that nothing in his artificial landscapes was ever left to chance. The highlights of the foregoing itinerary are once more displayed in quick succession: first the house, a few metres further on the PRAENESTE TERRACE, and then, one after the other, the two cascades in the VENUS VALE. Only now do we discern the spatial interrelationship of these scenes and discover that the PRAENESTE TERRACE reposes on arcades of Mediterranean appearance. These, in their turn, form a terrace that presents the finest view of the garden, leading the eye across a bend in the river and out into the open countryside. Here, beneath Kent's arcades, surrounded by classical-looking landscape scenes, we finally reach Arcadia.

The path disappears once more into the wood, which harbours some more small buildings, and ends by bringing us back to the *Bowling Green*. We now approach it from the other side – not necessarily any wiser than before (as the owl beneath the sculpted head seems to suggest), but most agreeably entertained by an ideal landscape which can be not only admired like a painting but traversed in person like the world itself.

Stourhead. View of the gardens
(watercolour by C. W. Bamphylde, 1775)

Aeneas in Wiltshire, or 'Et in Arcadia ego'

Stourhead, Wiltshire

English gardens play upon the expectant attitude of those who walk round them, transforming them into spectators of a landscape *mise en scène.* Meandering paths act as aids to these 'theatrical' productions. Travellers' impressions of the Grand Tour and landscape painters' compositions were Kent's principal theme. But the landscape gardener's rules of composition also lent themselves to telling stories which visitors, on their prescribed circuit of a garden, were intended to reconstruct in their imagination.

In the eighteenth century, walking round an English garden was quite commonly compared to reading a book. As Prince Pückler, the distinguished German landscape gardener, put it: 'A perfect park, or, in other words, an area idealized by art, should resemble a good book in *arousing* as many new ideas and emotions as it expresses.' Anyone who traverses an artificial landscape is at once a reader and a literary hero. He learns not only what has befallen others; he experiences it himself. Nowhere has this capacity of the landscape garden been more consistently fulfilled than at Stourhead.

Kent had set greater store at Chiswick on imitating antiquity than on imitating Nature, whereas at Rousham their roles were reversed. At Stourhead, both are on a par.

At least, that used to be the case. One of Stourhead's later owners remarked that he had no love for 'nature over-crowded with buildings'. Buildings were demolished and additional trees planted. Stourhead has been a paradise for dendrologists and lovers of rhododendron bushes since the nineteenth century. However, much of this luxuriant vegetation should be mentally deleted by anyone wishing to picture the original Stourhead itinerary.

The banker Henry Hoare had built a country house with Palladian features here back in 1717. His son, another Henry and a banker likewise, retired to Stourhead at the age of thirty-six. Henry Hoare II (1705–85), who had also undertaken the Grand Tour, returned to England in 1741. Soon afterwards he embarked on the design of his garden, an enclosed and entirely self-sufficient work of the landscaper's art isolated from the surrounding district by hills. It was completely independent of the house, and no gardens had previously existed there. Hoare incorporated the village and its medieval church in his referential system of angles of view and visual effects.

The first thing that strikes the eye as one enters the gardens is a brilliant white PANTHEON. In order to reach it, visitors must undertake a two-mile circuit of the lake, during which they will be greeted by a series of landscape impressions, architectural quotations and literary allusions. The PANTHEON's reference to antiquity is complemented by a TEMPLE OF FLORA with four Tuscan colums and a circular TEMPLE OF APOLLO. All three buildings become visible at precisely calculated moments. These views transmit what might be called a complex system of messages: a text whose decipherment entails a certain degree of educational background. Thus, the TEMPLE OF FLORA (the first stop on a walk round the lake) bears the following inscription: *'Procul, O procul este, profani'* (Begone, O begone, ye uniniated). The Sybil addresses those words to Aeneas when he enters the Underworld (in Book IV of the *Aeneid*).

Scholars have spent decades wrangling over the potential layers of meaning inherent in Henry Hoare's erudition-packed garden programme. Visitors to this artificial world need not be concerned by this, however, because each experiences whatever becomes apparent to him. (That is as much a characteristic of the landscape garden as it is of any book.) And Henry Hoare employed all manner of allusions to ensure that people understood the story he wished to tell.

His first step was to dam the river Stour (to which the place owes its name) in order to create the lake, the heart of the gardens. He was assisted in designing the buildings by Henry Flitcroft, a protégé of Lord Burlington and friend of William Kent. The TEMPLE OF FLORA, completed in 1746, was originally dedicated to Ceres, the ancient goddess of grain and harvest. The PANTHEON (1753/4) was at first called the TEMPLE OF HERCULES. In addition to Hercules, whose association with garden design stemmed from his theft of the golden apples of the Hesperides, it contains statues of Flora, the goddess of gardens, Diana, the goddess of hunting, and the Egyptian goddess Isis. It seems that Henry Hoare's initial concern was to illustrate the new ties with Nature by means of mythological allusions, and to use his garden to revive various forms of devotion to it.

This is further suggested by the visual relationship between the Christian village church and the temples dedicated to the Nature worship of the ancient world. But church and temples are also symbolic of moral authority, and it was not long before Nature worship yielded pride of place at Stourhead to honorific sculptural tributes to exalted heroes. In addition to Hercules, our circuit of the lake takes us past King Alfred and several statues of Aeneas of Troy, whose years-long odyssey ended in Italy, where his descendants founded Rome. And that this landscape is pervaded by the spirit of Rome becomes clear at first glance.

Anyone standing in front of the TEMPLE OF FLORA will see the TEMPLE OF APOLLO on the left, on the other side of the lake, and the PANTHEON on the right. The route to the PANTHEON leads first through some sparse broadleaved trees, but these soon give way to conifers of increasing density. The path runs downhill, flanked by boulders. At its lowest point, almost level with the surface of the lake, it comes to a stone archway beyond which can be heard the mysterious sound of rushing water. It is cool, dark and damp down there. We descend still further into a small grotto chamber in which a nymph reclines in front of a gushing spring. An opening in the stonework discloses a view across the lake. In this mysterious sphere of the underworld we come upon another quotation from Virgil's *Aeneid.* Further along this subterranean serpentine, we are suddenly confronted by a river god with water seething round him. His raised hand and extended forefinger point the way up a narrow flight of stone steps and out of the grotto. The sound of water gradually fades, the conifer plantation thins once more, the scenery becomes more cheerful, more open and lighter.

Beyond one bend in the path we sight the majestic colonnaded façade of the PANTHEON, and beyond another the whole of that brilliant white building. From here, the gardens' architectural and spiritual centrepiece, we get an unobstructed view across the lake with the sky reflected in it. Spanning a lateral arm of the river on the opposite bank is a graceful five-arched bridge (modeled on a bridge at Vicenza designed by Palladio) flanked by the TEMPLE OF APOLLO and the TEMPLE OF FLORA. The rounded, curving stretches of bank on either side of the PANTHEON itself soon give way to more rugged scenery if we continue along our route. Passing a cascade, we come to a flight of a rugged stone steps and then climb steeply until we reach the TEMPLE OF APOLLO (whose highly original design is based on a temple at Baalbek). This marks the climax of the dramaturgical programme as well as the gardens' highest geographical point. From here – and only here – we can survey the whole of the landscape we have just traversed. In order to gain a full view and understanding of the gardens' complex design, however, we must first have completed the separate stages of the route.

Also visible at a distance in earlier times was a massive tower in the Gothic style: ALFRED'S TOWER. Henry Hoare erected this after 1762 to commemorate the end of the Seven Years' War with France and pay homage to George III, who had ascended the British throne two years earlier. In contrast to his two predecessors of the same name, who had concentrated on pursuing Hanover's interests

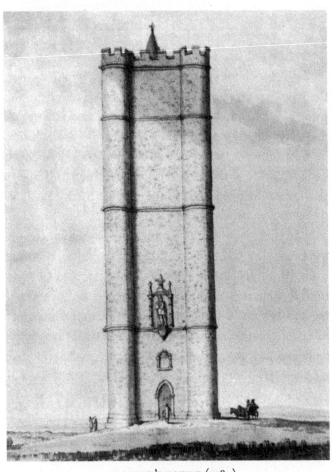

ALFRED'S TOWER (1784)

and embroiled Great Britain in all kinds of military con-
flicts, George III aspired to be 'a truly British King' – like
his predecessor Alfred the Great (871–99), who drove out
the Danes and codified Anglo-Saxon laws, thereby earning
himself the reputation of being the real founder of the

Claude Lorrain:
Aeneas in Delos (1672)

British constitution. An inscription on the tower, intended as a tribute to both men, reads: 'The Father of his People / The Founder of the English Monarchy and Liberty'. A twelfth-century chronicle identifies Aeneas as an ancestor of the Britons, so ALFRED'S TOWER may also, at least loosely, be incorporated in Stourhead's heroic programme.

It is clear that Aeneas's career and its various stages in the *Aeneid* play a key role in our understanding of the gardens, but there his journey through life is topicalized: in contact with the political situation and contemporary culture, the old story acquires new significance. Various pointers make it clear to visitors that *they* are following in Aeneas's footsteps. There are also two allusions to the *Aeneid* which require some knowledge of art history: the river god who indicates the way out of the grotto is closely modelled on a print by Salvator Rosa entitled *Tiber and Aeneas,* and the whole garden seems to be freely based on a celebrated picture by the landscape painter Claude Lorrain. Now in London's National Gallery, it shows *Aeneas in Delos.* In the foreground we discern the Tuscan columns of the TEMPLE OF FLORA, in the background another temple not unlike the PANTHEON at Stourhead. Stretching away on the left is the sea, which at Stourhead has become a lake. The relative positions of the garden buildings more or less accord with those in the painting, except that Henry Hoare opened the picture out. The charm of the gardens lies in the structuring of the spaces between the temples and the transposition of Claude Lorrain's painting – and its literary model – into three dimensions. Lorrain painted an idealized picture of antiquity. Thanks to Henry Hoare, we can visit it in person.

Thomas Daniell:
West Wycombe, south front (1781)

Palladio four times over and a trip across the Styx,
or the triumph of the Dilettanti

West Wycombe, Buckinghamshire

Political ideals and social utopias were not the only things that could be staged in a garden setting with the techniques developed at Rousham, Stourhead and elsewhere. The direction in which he guided the visitor's imagination through his artificial landscape was entirely up to the individual owner. At West Wykeham, Sir Francis Dashwood (1708–81) demonstrated that the modern combination of man-made 'natural' scenery and garden temples was also suited to creating an appropriate setting for exuberant *joie de vivre* and sensual pleasure. In Dashwood's classicistic, idealized landscape, beauty is allied not only with truth and goodness but, above all, with what is pleasurable and entertaining.

Sir Francis inherited the house and estate in 1726. In the same year he embarked on a Grand Tour, which became the first of a whole series of trips abroad. In 1726 he visited France, Italy and Germany; in 1729 and 1731 he revisited Italy; in 1733 he obeyed an urge to visit Russia. This was a novelty, for Dashwood's diary contains the earliest descriptions of Moscow and St Petersburg in the English language. In 1735 he went to Greece and Asia Minor, and his last visit to Italy spanned the years 1739–41. Back home again, Dashwood spent twenty years in Parliament and served as Postmaster General from 1765 until his death. Benjamin Franklin, a frequent guest of Sir Francis, wrote of his visits to West Wycombe: 'The gardens are a paradise. But the pleasanter thing is the kind countenance and the facetious and very intelligent conversation of mine host, who, having been for many years engaged in public affairs, seen all parts of Europe and kept the very best company in the world, is himself the best existing.'

Between his trip to Greece and his last tour of Italy, Sir Frances began to redesign his house and gardens. Having collected sufficient material on his travels, he aspired to recreate the loveliest places in the world for his own benefit and that of his friends. Instead of demolishing the old house, he completely revamped it in the modern style: it was to be Palladian. The north front (whose design he entrusted to one of Lord Burlington's draughtsmen) was completed in 1751. Then came the splendid south front, with its two superposed colonnades, which was based on Palladio's Palazzo Chiericati at Vicenza. On the east and west fronts Dashwood added porticos (of which the former, like Lord Burlington's Chiswick House, is a quotation from the Villa Rotonda). He ended up with a country house possessing four Palladian showpiece façades, and in time the surrounding gardens, too, acquired a suitably Mediterranean aura.

The interior of the house was also italianized. To that end, Sir Frances had returned from one of his trips accompanied by a painter named Giuseppe Mattia Borgnis. After Borgnis's death his son took over the task of transforming West Wycombe into his patron's idea of a Mediterranean villa.

Sir Francis wanted a hall like a Roman atrium, so its walls were painted to resemble marble and pierced to connect it with the adjoining rooms. He also erected columns and statues and installed underfloor heating of the kind he had seen in Rome. Henry Hoare's heroes were Hercules, King Alfred and Aeneas; Sir Francis invested in Bacchus, Venus and Apollo.

Anyone entering the 'atriumized' hall will at once – even if entirely unaware of it – be drawn into their world. There are no less than three copies of the *Venus de' Medici* at West Wycombe: one on the staircase, one beneath the dome of the Temple of Venus in the garden, and one in a niche in the dining room that adjoins the hall on the right. Mounted in a niche facing it on the left of the hall is a mirror, so anyone setting foot in the hall will pass between Venus and her reflection and – this is doubtless the intended message – fall under the spell of the goddess of love. The house and garden have other, clearer pointers in store for the benefit of all who fail to grasp this subtle arrangement. The staircase is adorned with murals of biblical and mythological scenes based on Italian originals. The higher one climbs and the nearer the bedrooms, the more unmistakably erotic they become. Dashwood scattered the house and gardens with erotic motifs, favouring portrayals of his household deity, Bacchus, in company with his wife Ariadne. He also had the west portico of the house modelled on a temple of Bacchus, his intention being that house and gardens should merge to form an indissoluble whole.

The same idea also played a part in the design of the largest and most magnificent room in the house, the

West Wycombe, with the cascade in the foreground and the
church on the hill in the background
(engraving after William Hannan)

MUSIC ROOM. This affords a view of the most elaborate
of Dashwood's garden buildings, a classical temple set on
an idyllic island in an artificial lake. Dedicated to music,
it was used as a concert and banqueting hall. Just as the
Pantheon dominates the world of Stourhead as a symbol
of the heroes of Rome, so the TEMPLE OF MUSIC dominates the gardens of West Wycombe as a place of enjoyment. The central window on the garden side of the MUSIC
ROOM can be opened, together with the panelling, to enable
one to walk straight out into the open air. Surrounded by
Venus and Bacchus, with the MUSIC ROOM behind and the
TEMPLE OF MUSIC ahead, visitors were intended to roam
the agreeable landscape and enjoy it.

West Wycombe. In the background on the left, the house;
on the right, the TEMPLE OF VENUS
(engraving after William Hannan)

Apollo, too, has a temple devoted to him – an imposing
triumphal arch containing a copy of the *Belevedere Apollo*.
There is also a ROUND TEMPLE (which is not round but
creates that impression), a cascade with water nymphs, a
TEMPLE OF DAPHNE, a TEMPLE OF FLORA, and a TEMPLE
OF THE WINDS based on the Tower of the Winds in
Athens. Sir Francis always made the completion of garden
buildings an occasion for elaborate parties and torchlight
processions for which everyone had to wear fancy dress.

He also incorporated the countryside beyond the
gardens in the staging of his ideal landscape. In 1752
he heightened the tower of West Wycombe church, which
stands on a hill on the far side of the village street, and
topped it with a gold ball like the one he had seen on the

old customs house in Venice. In the course of these alterations, the nave was refaced in the style of ancient temples at Palmyra and Damascus, so the village church itself became a garden temple. Erected in 1764, a mausoleum on the edge of a graveyard serves as an additional eye-catcher when seen from the gardens. Whether for the sake of this distant visual effect or from sheer megalomania, the dimensions of this tomb and monument are enormous. An imposing edifice inspired by the Arch of Constantine in Rome, it could genuinely be mistaken for an ancient monument. The octagonal wall encloses an expanse of grass resembling a Roman archaeological site. At its centre stands a square temple surmounting an urn. Dashwood's tombstone bears the inscription: 'Revered, Respected and Beloved by all who knew him.'

The master of West Wycombe enlisted advice on his building activities from the Society of Dilettanti, an association founded in 1732 by a group of enthusiastic Grand Tourists centred on Sir Francis himself (it is still active today). It was an arts club for the cultural elite who had travelled to Italy and wished to promote a feeling for the cultural achievements of the ancient world. The society dispatched artists and architects to Italy and Greece, financed excavations at Herculaneum (1738) and Pompeii (1748), and sponsored literary projects such *The Antiquities of Athens,* a standard work by James Stewart and Nicholas Revett (1762–94). Horace Walpole wrote of the society that the nominal qualification for membership was having been in Italy and the real one being drunk. He added that its two most prominent members, Lord Middlesex and Sir

Francis Dashwood, had 'seldom been sober' during their sojourns in Italy.

During the eighteenth century, the term dilettante was far from being tainted with the disrespect which is our immediate response to it today. The dilettante was an alert and interested contemporary who appropriated the spirit and form of cultural highlights and creatively reproduced them as best he could. Englishmen must have sat sketching on every other street corner in Rome at this period. Others conveyed their impressions through the medium of poems and essays or, more commonly, in travel diaries and letters, many of which were published. While not of decisive importance to highlights and artistic profundity, dilettantism was all the more vital to the dissemination of culture in the eighteenth century. The dilettanti practised all the arts from writing and drawing to music and, especially in gardens, architecture. The dilettante's desire to resurrect antiquity back home made a substantial contribution to the development of the English garden. Dilettanti were the real experts on landscape gardening, which derived its motifs from all the arts. In this respect, a feeling for landscape painting was as helpful as a knowledge of literature and a basic knowledge of architecture. There were no professional landscape gardeners when the first landscape gardens originated, and no designer of an important garden, apart from Lord Burlington, was an architect.

That the dilettanti should have formed a society was far from extraordinary. The eighteenth century was also a heyday for clubs, associations and circles, in which England was particularly abundant. Anything considered important or worthy of encouragement could provide the reason for founding an association. There were small, private associations like Walpole's Committee of Taste and influential societies like the Kit-Kat Club. Most important of all were the political clubs in which like-minded individuals banded together for mutual support. Dashwood was not only instrumental in founding the Society of Dilettanti; he also initiated the Divan Club, a counterpart intended for those who had visited the Ottoman Empire and were interested in its culture. Finally, he founded the Hell Fire Club, which began life as The Knights of St Francis of Wycombe. That association combined the ingenious staging of Dashwoodian *joie de vivre* with the clubs' elitist pretensions and political commitment. Many members who opposed the government joined circles of which some assumed the character of secret societies. All the Knights of St Francis of Wykeham belonged to an opposition circle centred on Frederick, Prince of Wales. The society's establishment was additionally coloured by the profound contempt for the Roman Catholic Church, which Dashwood had cultivated during his sojourns in Italy. (To manifest that sentiment, he posed for William Hogarth attired as a Franciscan monk and gazing lustfully at a recumbent statuette of Venus.) The secretary of the Hell Fire Club was the writer Paul Whitehead, whose acquaintance Sir Francis had made at the Sublime Society of Beefsteaks. Nobody knows exactly what went on when the members, dressed in monks' habits, met at night. All that is known is how much they drank. A cellar book carefully records how many bottles of wine were sunk by each of the twelve 'brothers'. Women were admitted, but only – to quote the society's statutes – if their 'agreeable and lively disposition' contributed to the general good cheer. The meeting place was a Cistercian abbey beside the Thames to which Dashwood devoted almost as much effort as he did to the creation of his landscape garden. However, the club is also said to have convened in the HELLFIRE CAVES, a system of caves beneath West Wycombe church, which are among the more bizarre sensations of the English Garden Tour. Writing to Philadelphia in 1772, Benjamin Franklin stated that His Lordship's ideas, which made a rather weird and whimsical impression, were just as manifest below the ground as above it.

In the 1740s, when a shaft was being driven into the hill below the church to extract building material for a new road, Sir Francis could not resist exploiting this unique opportunity to create a dramatic representation of the Underworld. The cave system is entered by way of a forecourt to which he lent the appearance of a ruined medieval monastery. Seen from the house, these fragmentary walls and gable ends, which were erected around 1750, really could be mistaken for a dilapidated ancient monument. Behind this dummy façade an underground passage runs into the hillside for over a quarter of a mile. It is not known whether Dashwood based the design of his subterranean world on a pre-existing pattern or whether he was simply playing around with old shapes to which magical significance was attributed. The underground chambers form a ring, a labyrinth, a triangle, and a circle. Halfway along is a banqueting hall with a domed roof. The passage not only leads deeper and deeper into the hillside but runs steadily downhill. Nearly a hundred metres beneath the church, visitors come to the conclusion and objective of their truly eerie journey into the unknown: the INNER TEMPLE. Separating this from the passage is an underground stream which, like the mythical river that divides the world from the underworld, bears the name STYX. Two hundred and fifty years ago, following the mythical example, a boat was kept here for crossing the STYX. Of all representations of the underworld in eighteenth-century gardens, the HELLFIRE CAVES of West Wykeham are undoubtedly the most impressive.

Hendrik de Cort:
Castle Howard (c. 1800)

*The attractions of space, or how a
village street became a terrace*

Castle Howard, Yorkshire

C ountry estates began to change their appearance at
the outset of the eighteenth century, not only in the
vicinity of London but in other parts of England as well
– Yorkshire, for example. There, too, the inexorable geom-
etry of garden design lost the force of law, and there, too,
friends and neighbours exchanged advice and influenced
one another when treading new paths in garden design.
However, it seems that what first exploded aesthetic conventions and overstepped the usual boundaries was less
a feeling for Nature than a love of size and the desire to
impress neighbours, guests, and visitors with something
unprecedented. After all, country seats have always been
status symbols as well as residences. As houses increased in
size, so did the gardens surrounding them, and the bigger
they were the more exposed they became to their natural
surroundings. To enhance the impression of scale and
extent, designers incorporated the countryside beyond the
garden boundaries in their sketches. Conversely, the boundary between the controlled art of the garden and the open
countryside also became permeable: anyone wishing to
create an unbroken transition between a designed garden
and its undesigned surroundings was compelled to take

Castle Howard c. 1725

account, however cautiously, of the irregularity and boundlessness that characterizes untouched Nature.

Whereas in the South of England the desire for naturalness in a garden preceded the staging of a new sense of space, precisely the opposite occurred in Yorkshire, where some of the most magnificent gardens came into being between Baroque and Enlightenment. There, wealthy and ambitious estate owners wanted to dramatize the space surrounding their country mansions as effectively as possible.

The earliest and most impressive such example is the Howard family's country seat near York. There, from 1700 onwards, one of the biggest English Baroque gardens came into being. Every conceivable superlative of 'big' is applicable to this house and the artificial landscape surrounding it. The only boundary that remained in the end was the horizon. Horace Walpole, who visited Castle Howard in August 1777, was bowled over by it. No one, he wrote, had prepared him for the sight of a palace, a village and a fortified town all in one. He rhapsodized about the lofty temples, the woods, of which each could have been a druidical metropolis, the valleys connected by woods and hills, the noble expanses of lawn, and a mausoleum that could tempt one to want to be buried alive in it. He had seen gigantic places before, but never one that was 'sublime'.

'Sublime' was *the* aesthetic buzzword of the eighteenth century, a term collectively applied by philosophers and aesthetes to all those shapes and objects that rejoiced the eye without being compatible with the classical canon of beauty and its basic rules. Foremost among these were irregular, sometimes rugged natural shapes, but also an impression of boundless space. Hitherto, everything too vast or 'untidy' for the human eye to take in and sort out had tended to be excluded from the realm of art. That did not change until art began to conquer Nature after 1700. In this respect, the concept of 'sublimity' was of vital importance. Nature has its own laws, among which are irregularity, the contrast between different areas, and the absence of boundaries. Sublimity became established as the complementary alternative to classical beauty. In landscape gardens, symmetrical structure, visual clarity and distinct boundaries were replaced by an alternation of different moods, surprise effects that overwhelmed the visitor, and the skilful presentation of the boundlessness of Nature.

The sublime effect of Castle Howard depends mainly on the last of these. The word 'sublime' was already on everyone's lips when Walpole visited Yorkshire in 1777, but not when Charles Howard, 3rd Earl of Carlisle, inherited Henderskelfe Castle in 1692. He was assisted in redesigning his family seat by two men: John Vanbrugh and Nicholas Hawksmoor.

Sir John Vanbrugh is said to have had the idea of becoming an architect during his three years in the Bastille as a prisoner of the French. On his release, however, he first tried his luck as a playwright, and he never lost his penchant for the theatrical as an architect. His architectural designs combined this with a no less pronounced tendency towards gigantomania. 'Beautiful' is not really the word for these huge, bombastic buildings. When Henderskelfe Castle burned down in 1693, Vanbrugh soon came up with a visionary design for its replacement. Although he had plenty of ideas, he had never built a house before, so the professional assistance of the architect Nicholas Hawksmoor was enlisted and Carlisle himself, being the ultimate authority, supervised all plans relating to the redesign of his country seat.

Work on the new house began in 1700. Vanbrugh set about his task wholly encumbered by architectural traditions, in fact Jonathan Swift poked fun at him on that account: 'Van's genius, without thought or lecture, / is hugely turn'd to architecture.' He adhered neither to the customary east-west axis nor to a uniform style. Above all, though, his grand visions, surprisingly many of which were put into effect, required an immense amount of space. The old castle had been situated between the church and the main road in the village of Henderskelfe. Vanbrugh wanted an entirely free hand in this area. The village stood in his way, so it was demolished. As for the former village street, Carlisle and Vanbrugh later made it a component of their design for the gardens and grounds.

For the new castle Vanbrugh designed miles-long, dead straight approach roads that attune the visitor to his aesthetic of the grandiose long before they reach the entrance. This implacably straight line traverses hill and dale, cuts through woods and copses, and eventually debouches into an imposing avenue of lime trees. Elaborate gate buildings provide a foretaste of the magnificence beyond them, and a stout wall punctuated by eleven towers of different design creates the impression of a heavily fortified bastion. Rising from the centre of this wall is Vanbrugh's massive GATEHOUSE, topped with a pyramid, to which side wings were added in 1756 to accommodate garden tourists. For

Castle Howard's fame attracted many visitors to Yorkshire. Their response filled Vanbrugh with satisfaction. Everyone was most surprised and impressed by the walls and their towers, he wrote, and he had always felt sure that they represented 'a trump card'.

The most outstanding feature of Castle Howard's architecture is its monumentality. Vanbrugh did not build, he was an architectural stage manager, and he always stage-managed the same thing: size. Various artists contributed to the interior decoration, among them William Kent. Vanbrugh himself took responsibility for the central space, the hall, whose arches, niches, columns and galleries are surmounted by an enormous dome. The latter was not originally provided for. When the decision to erect a dome was taken, it became the biggest that had ever presided over any English country house.

That the west wing had not been built by the time of Vanbrugh's death in 1726 was attributable less to financial constraints than to the fact that Carlisle had become more interested in the surroundings of his new house than in the building itself. In 1710 Vanbrugh had designed an enormous garden in the French style. We do not know how much of it was actually completed. The regular parterre with an Atlas fountain in the middle, which now extends along the south front, dates from the latter half of the nineteenth century. The rose garden west of the house, with its remarkable assortment of old roses, was not created until the twentieth century. Castle Howard has always remained in the family's possession, and each succeeding generation has made its own contribution to its appearance.

Carlisle directed Vanbrugh's attention first to the eastern part of the grounds. There, paths laid through an area of woodland led past statues and fountains to an amphitheatre and some small summerhouses. This part of the gardens was much admired by eighteenth-century garden tourists, notably for its buildings and statuary. These have not, however, survived the passage of time. The small wood in the south was bounded by Henderskelfe's former village street, which had been deprived of its original function when the village was demolished. Carlisle and Vanbrugh converted it into a grass-covered terrace lined with statues. It follows its original course, so is neither entirely level nor straight. This mitigates the contrast between the artistry of the gardens and the naturalness of the landscape visible from there.

Below the terrace is a series of man-made water features, of which SOUTH LAKE still betrays the Baroque predilection for straightening banks. It ends in an artificial watercourse, the NEW RIVER, which forms a transition between the artificiality of the gardens and the open countryside. Since the 1740s the river has been spanned by the NEW RIVER BRIDGE (also known as the ROMAN BRIDGE on account of its classical design). Together with the meadows and fields surrounding them, river and bridge constitute an impressive sight, especially when seen from the SOUTH LAKE.

In other respects, and despite its gigantomania, Castle Howard presents a unified and harmonious picture. Wherever views of the countryside can be seen from the grounds, man-made garden landscape and untouched natural surroundings are skillfully attuned to each other. Carlisle instructed his architect to erect garden buildings outside the gardens as well. The whole of the surrounding countryside and the horizon beyond it are positively absorbed into the grounds. Erected on the edge of a field south-west of the park was a pyramid designed by Hawksmoor. Carlisle, who had a particular weakness for that shape, instructed his architects and gardeners to erect pyramids everywhere: on top of the entrance gates, on the paths across the garden parterres, on bridges and in open spaces. In 1729 Hawksmoor transmitted a message to the Earl from the future inheritor of Castle Howard: Lord Morpeth requested that his father deign to employ some ornaments in the park other than pyramids, he being of the opinion that there were enough of them already.

Vanbrugh died in 1726, just when Lord Burlington was at work on the plans for his Palladian villa at Chiswick. Vanbrugh's last design for Castle Howard, completed in the year of his death, was a Palladian TEMPLE OF THE WINDS, which forms the culmination of the long terrace that leads visitors from the castle into the landscape. By echoing the columns and dome of the house on a smaller scale, this temple creates the impression of an annexe, a garden room belonging to the castle itself. In this way, the grassy terrace is closely bonded with the architecture and helps to emphasize its magnitude. The principal justifications for the temple's existence are its location and the view it affords, which is one of the most magnificent presented by any English landscape garden. In the east, south and west it stretches away over fields, valleys and woods to the horizon, and the picture is rounded off in every direction by a building: in the middle by the NEW RIVER BRIDGE; on the right by Hawksmoor's pyramid; and on the left by the Howard family's mausoleum (whose splendour tempted Walpole to want to be buried alive there). Hawksmoor designed the pyramid and this tomb, which is thoroughly in keeping with the dimensions of the whole place, in 1728/9, but it was not completed until 1744. Carlisle, who had died in 1738, is said to have declared that one should only design and start work on great palaces, leaving it to posterity to complete them by degrees.

Anthony Walker: Studley Royal.
BANQUETING HOUSE and rotunda (1758)

Studley Royal, Yorkshire

At studley royal near Ripon, not far from Castle Howard, experiments in garden design were prompted not by the space available but by proximity to a formal park. John Aislabie (1670–1742), who inherited the property in 1699, was a friend of Lord Burlington and Sir John Vanbrugh. He was also an ambitious man who quickly attained high office in the Whig administration. In 1716 he began to create a garden at Studley Royal. Ponds and canals were excavated, artificial hills thrown up and cascades installed at enormous expense. At various times, hundreds of seasonal workers were employed on earth-moving operations. Big, symmetrical expanses of lawn and water features of geometrical design took shape. However, certain features typical of French Baroque gardens were absent. The garden was not directly related to the house (which burned down in 1946), nor are there any of the customary parterres complete with flower beds and borders. Also missing is a central axis, which formed the backbone of a French garden's geometrical patterns.

This resulted from Aislabie's unusual decision to adapt his garden to the natural characteristics of the site. He centred it on the river Skell, not on an avenue or canal. Thus the park is not an artificial construction designed on the drawing board, but an expanse of artistically modified landscape. Although Aislabie canalized the river and altered the character of the terrain with geometrical lawns, pools, hedges, and paths, the course of the river and valley continued to govern the shape of his garden, whose strict formalism presents a rather weird contrast to the dense, dark green woods that flank the valley on either side.

All work on the garden was suspended in December 1720, and Aislabie did not resume it until six years later, when he settled at Studley Royal for good. This was not because of his involvement with the political opposition, but the result of a disastrous financial operation. Aislabie fell prey to one of the greatest economic scandals of the age: he was one of the leading backers of the South Sea Company. Owing to its inglorious collapse at the time of the notorious 'South Sea Bubble', he not only lost a great deal of money but forfeited his parliamentary seat as well. He was even temporarily imprisoned in the Tower and disqualified for life from public office. Embittered by this fiasco, he retired to Studley Royal and devoted himself entirely to his garden thereafter.

Aislabie's composition also incorporated antique statues and temples connected by a network of visual axes. The finest garden building at Studley Royal is a Greek temple in the Doric style. Set against the dark woods in the background and reflected in a circular pond, this stands beside a curving, semicircular stretch of lawn. The scene is further enlivened by statues of Bacchus, Neptune and Endymion. Erected in 1740, the temple was originally dedicated to Hercules like the PANTHEON at Stourhead. Aislabie's son

William renamed it the TEMPLE OF PIETY in memory of his father, who had died in 1742.

William was a member of Parliament like his parent. Unlike him, he had been on the Grand Tour (in 1720, the year that had proved so disastrous to his family). Garden design in England had undergone a change by the time he inherited Studley Royal. Kent was currently engaged in transforming the park at Rousham into a charming ideal landscape, Henry Hoare starting work at Stourhead on his artificial world inspired by literature. William Aislabie actively participated in the new fashion. He left his father's buildings and ponds as they were, likewise the straightened river, but added buildings and paths and expanded the park, transforming Studley Royal into a landscape garden. He extended the landscaping of the Skell valley to the north-east, where it narrows to form a rocky, romantic gorge. William threaded this with paths that set off the river and rocks for the benefit of those who make their way along them. He also erected various garden buildings (not all of which have survived). The gorge derived its name – SEVEN BRIDGES WALK – from the seven bridges that span the river. It now presents the naturalistic appearance especially prized during the late eighteenth and nineteenth centuries: varied, pristine, and sometimes a trifle harsh and rugged. Today we would call it 'beautiful' or possibly 'romantic'; it was then considered 'sublime'.

William Aislabie had a special affinity with 'sublime Nature'. At Hackfall, a few miles from Studley Royal, he had prefaced the addition of SEVEN BRIDGES WALK to his father's garden by transforming a shadowy, rocky gorge into a small landscape garden devoted entirely to presenting Nature in its 'sublime' form; that is to say, he eschewed the charm of bright, pleasant scenery in favour of the dark and rugged, gloomy and dramatic. Architecturally, Aislabie underlined that mood by means of an octagonal tower in Gothic guise, in other words, with a quotation from a style of architecture that was deemed to exert the same effects as Nature in the raw. After 1750, landscape gardens devoted more and more space to such presentations of the 'sublime': artificial rocks and waterfalls, dilapidated 'devil's bridges' and Gothic ruins in gloomy woods abounded. Nature seemed particularly natural in such settings, and the semblance of naturalness had became the garden designer's supreme commandment. Although truly 'wild' gardens like Aislabie's Hackfall remained something of a rarity, similar settings soon became part of the English garden designer's stock in trade. (Very little survives of Hackfall, whose exploration is a task for the genuine expert.)

The 'sublime' effects of Studley Royal also include the south-west end of the garden valley, where John Aislabie had created a view in no way inferior to Castle Howard's magnificent landscapes. Half a mile from the property's original boundary stands one of Britain's most impressive ruins: Fountains Abbey, the remains of a twelfth-century Cistercian monastery. It is the most complete and best-preserved Cistercian abbey in the country. John Aislabie, who set store by his view of the ruin, had had the idea of incorporating Fountains Abbey in his garden. Negotiations to that end failed in 1720, however, so he had to content himself with a distant view of his object of desire. It was left to William Aislabie to fulfill his father's dream. In 1768 he acquired the ruin for £16,000. It had been going for £4000 in his father's day, but the demand for all things Gothic had boomed in the meantime.

'Ruins appear best at a distance,' noted the travel writer Arthur Young. This observation may have consoled John Aislabie when nothing came of his attempt to purchase Fountains Abbey. However, William Aislabie's acquisition of the site enabled him to make a garden attraction not of the view of the impressive monument but of the ruin itself. Medieval ruins, which could do more than intact Gothic buildings to enhance the effect of rugged landscape impressions, became a standard component of 'sublime' garden scenery. Ruins symbolized Nature's triumph over civilization. Furthermore, incomplete walls spurred the imagination. People had to visualize the missing sections of ancient buildings and could picture what had gone on within them. Thrillers in line of descent from Horace Walpole's *The Castle of Otranto* supplied material for such imaginings, it being of secondary importance whether ruined walls were genuinely old or only appeared so.

Today, the circuit of Studley Royal leads from the man-made lake at the north end of the valley and along the canalized river to Fountains Abbey, passing John Aislabie's formal gardens, statues and temples. The HIGH PATH, an uneven path that leads through the woods above the formal gardens, begins at the OCTAGON TOWER, which was originally built in the classical style but subsequently gothicized. The highlight of this gently ascending route is a spot that has rightly been christened the SURPRISE VIEW.

Anthony Walker: Studley Royal.
View of the park with Fountains Abbey in the background (1758)

This presents a magnificent, wholly unexpected, slightly elevated view of Fountains Abbey. Our eye is drawn to the far-off building in company with our imagination. Because of our distance from it, but mainly because of the difference in altitude and the direction in which the path continues, the ruin seems unattainable. This is another determinant of the visual axes in a landscape garden, which are invariably focused on buildings and places whose location renders us uncertain when or whether we will reach them.

After 1768, William Aislabie had an opportunity to extend the path as far as the ruin itself. He made the approach to Fountains Abbey as exciting and effective as possible, employing techniques which the art of landscape gardening had evolved in the interim. Restorers have taken a lot of trouble to reproduce the original planting of this path along the river, because the trees and undergrowth provide for suspense and a number of unexpected views. The ruin is mostly out of sight, the trees permitting only occasional glimpses of its walls. It presents a different appearance every time because the path's twists and turns produce differing lines of sight. On rounding one bend, for example, we get a view of the monastery's east face. It is quite close, but the river still separates us from our goal and the path disappears into the trees once more. Although the ruin is even closer the next time we see it, we are again compelled to redirect our gaze by a hairpin bend. The next bend yields another surprise: instead of being confronted by the massive, looming walls of the abbey, we come out into a big field strewn with ruins: foundation walls, the remains of a staircase, a truncated column lying in the grass. We can readily conceive that Grand Tourists like William Aislabie were reminded by this of ruined sites in Italy. Overgrown with grass, the projecting walls must have been reminiscent of Roman archaeological sites they had seen on their visits to Italy and of the vestiges of antiquity they so revered. In this instance, however, the foundation walls are those of the abbey infirmary. Crossing this expanse of ruins, we come at last to the abbey church itself, with its north tower and roofless nave, its lofty arches and massive piers. Our circuit of Studley Royal's landscape garden culminates in an exploration of the sublime ruins of Fountains Abbey, a marvel of medieval architecture whose dilapidated remains exude a very special charm. The path through William Aislabie's garden, with its abundance of suspense and surprise effects, is the finest possible preparation for that experience.

Duncombe House (c. 1725)

When pictures learnt to walk, or a
short history of the terrace

Duncombe and Rievaulx
Terrace, Yorkshire

The unusual gardens of Castle Howard and Studley
Royal possess a neighbour in the immediate vicinity: Duncombe. A terrace there is reminiscent of Castle
Howard, while the ruins of a medieval Cistercian monastery remind one of Studley Royal.

In 1713, Thomas Duncombe II began to redesign his
country seat (which bears his name). He probably enlisted
the advice of John Vanbrugh, who was then engaged with
the construction of Castle Howard.

The land behind Duncombe House falls away steeply. By
a considerable stretch of the imagination, the terrain could
put one in mind of the celebrated terraces of Tivoli, one
of the obligatory ports of call for contemporary visitors to
Italy. This was what inspired Thomas Duncombe to recreate Tivoli in Yorkshire. Following the natural contours
of the summit of the hill, he laid out a grassy terrace there
– ten years before Carlisle and Vanbrugh converted the
former village street of Henderskelfe Castle into a similar
attraction. At both ends of this terrace he erected temples
modeled on Tivoli's celebrated Temples of Vesta and the
Sibyl. One was completed around 1718, possibly after a

design by Vanbrugh, while the other was probably based on the mausoleum at Castle Howard.

Having been enchanted by Tivoli and other historic terraced towns, many British visitors drew their inspiration from them when they became landscape gardeners back home. At Rousham, for example, the garden's sloping position suggested a similar construction – one that would combine a view of the landscape with memories of the Grand Tour. As time went by, however, terraces in English gardens became rarer because architectural interference with the landscape was too apparent and spoilt the illusion of naturalness.

Terraces are among the earliest elements of garden design. Originally an agricultural device designed to render hilly terrain cultivable, they became a formative ornament and vantage point in Italian Renaissance gardens. Terraces also played an important role in French Baroque gardens. While Louis XIV was awaiting the completion of Versailles at Saint-Germain-en-Laye, his garden architect Le Nôtre created the aptly named GRANDE TERRASSE there. Dead straight and over two kilometres in length, this masterpiece (of engineering as well as garden design) opened up a new dimension in the conquest of Nature by architecture. Finally, in early landscape gardens, terraces were used as a means of staging a new experience of landscape space. Viewing terraces bound by balustrades became outsized ha-has that afforded spectacular views of the landscape, awakened memories of Italy, and, at the same time, replaced garden walls. This impression is also conveyed by the handsome, gently curving grassy terrace at Duncombe.

Not far from Duncombe House stand the ruins of Rievaulx Abbey, a Cistercian monastery. The remains of the medieval abbey's walls are romantically situated in the valley of the river Rye. Although the ruin is not quite as impressive as Fountains Abbey, it also presents an imposing sight, especially from the slopes that rise on either side of the Rye valley. Arthur Young's dictum – that 'ruins appear best at a distance' – is even more applicable to Rivaulx than to Fountains Abbey. Probably inspired by John Aislabie's grandiose interpretation of that remark at Studley Royal, Thomas Duncombe planned to create a second terrace overlooking the monastery walls, but he died before he could put that scheme into effect. Once again, it was left to Duncombe's son and successor to fulfil his father's intention. In the meantime, it had become a landscape gardener's ambition to produce impressive and surprising effects by means of an interplay between art, Nature and architecture. Thomas Duncombe III succeeded in creating one of the most original landscape gardens in the history of English garden design.

He set to work in 1758, or ten years before William Aislabie managed to purchase Fountains Abbey. In 1740 he had married Lady Diana Howard, one of the daughters of the owner of Castle Howard. Thus, he was well acquainted with Carlisle's and Vanbrugh's magnificent artificial landscape, its terrace included, and knew that there were no real limits to the possibility of creating impressive landscaping effects by artistic means. Duncombe's echoes of Tivoli were complemented by the laying of RIEVAULX TERRACE above the ruined monastery. Thomas Duncombe seems even to have planned to connect his two terraces by means of an enormous viaduct, so as to be able to present his guests with a long, continuous series of views over the Yorkshire country-side as they crossed it by carriage. This very idea makes it clear that, to landscape gardeners, no venture seemed too audacious and no plan too hybrid when it came to startling people with spectacular *mises en scène*.

One enters RIEVAULX TERRACE by the old gate through which Duncombe once drove with his guests. The grass-covered terrace of Rievaulx, too, follows the natural curve of the hill, and it, too, is bound by two classical temples. A circular temple, the TUSCAN TEMPLE, was erected at the south end in 1758. The splendid interior floor dates from the thirteenth century and was taken from the choir of Rievaulx Abbey. The temple steps afford an elevated view of the valley, in which the river is spanned by a bridge of medieval appearance. This was rebuilt after its predecessor was washed away by a flood in October 1754. The ruined monastery is still invisible – intentionally so, of course, because RIEVAULX TERRACE is not only a terrace but a garden path obedient to the landscape gardener's rules of dramatic composition. Like William Aislabie at Studley Royal, Thomas Duncombe designed it as a suspenseful approach to the sublime remains of the ancient monastery.

The terrace runs north for over half a mile. Our view of the valley is obscured by trees except where, at care-fully chosen points, Duncombe cut thirteen lanes through them. As we walk along the terrace, a series of thirteen dif-ferent views of the landscape unfolds. It is the beholder who moves, not the pictures he sees. This is one of the most important dramaturgical devices evolved by the new art of landscape gardening. At Rievaulx Thomas Duncombe successfully combined that principle with the old, architectonic conformation of the terrace. The effect he produced was, and is, unique.

Our first view of the bridge from the TUSCAN TEMPLE is succeeded by a series of views of the river valley, some of them enlivened by old farmhouses. Then, halfway along the terrace, the ruins of Rievaulx Abbey come into view for the first time – an impressive sight, and as unexpected as Studley Royal's SURPRISE VIEW. More views of the dilapidated walls follow. The curve of the terrace ensures that we always see them from a different angle and in front of a different background. The valley changes in appearance too, seeming to vary in width and framing the abbey's noble remains in a variety of ways. The proud nave looks particularly complete and majestic when glimpsed through the last of the thirteen lanes at the north end of the terrace, the highlight of this series of views. The IONIC TEMPLE at the end of the terrace path also conforms to a dramaturgy of intensification. This rectangular building (a copy of the Temple of Fortuna in the Forum Romanum) is bigger and more massive than the TUSCAN TEMPLE.

The interior of the temple has a final surprise in store: it contains a splendidly decorated and lavishly appointed banqueting room. The ceiling paintings are by Giuseppe Mattia Borgnis, the artist whom Sir Francis Dashwood brought back with him from Italy in 1751 and employed to transform his country house at West Wycombe into an Italian villa. Borgnis used some of the same motifs here, and he also imported the theme: like the east portico at West Wycombe, the ceiling depicts Apollo and the Muses, while the surrounding frieze is devoted to famous lovers from Greek mythology. It was here beneath their gaze that Thomas Duncombe invited his marveling guests to dine after walking along the terrace (meals were prepared in a kitchen housed in the base of the temple). This was where they returned to the present after their host had sent them on a brief journey through time and space by means of a series of views that had brought to life not only the cultural achievements of antiquity and the Mediterranean landscape, but the sublime architecture of the Gothic era. In an account of a tour of England published in 1771, Arthur Young rhapsodized about this extraordinary place for pages on end. He summarized his impression of it by saying that it had afforded him an unexpected glimpse of 'a little paradise' that looked as if it were situated in another world.

At Harewood Park, not far from Duncombe, another garden terrace can be inspected. This is of later date, however. Charles Barry, the architect of London's massive neo-Gothic Houses of Parliament, created it in the middle of the nineteenth century, when garden designers entertained a different idea of 'naturalization' from that which had inspired the exuberantly theatrical 'Men of Taste' and the Grand Tourists of the eighteenth century. After 1800, the effective interplay of art and nature that distinguished landscape gardeners of the first generation gave ground to a garden concept in which natural and artificial areas were deliberately divorced. In the so-called Pleasure Grounds around Harewood House, beds and borders, flower arrangements and sculptures mark the area where art reigns, whereas the extensive parkland adjoining the Pleasure Grounds creates a fluid transition to open countryside. The assembling of original miniature copies of various landscape scenes and architectural monuments within a small compass gives way to a cultivation of landscape that once more respects and emphasizes the boundary between art and Nature.

Prior to this, however, the plan to eliminate that boundary altogether was taken to a pitch of perfection. Garden buildings lost their importance. Ingenious appeals to the imagination were replaced by a desire to create artificial landscapes indistinguishable from Nature, except that they were intended to be more consummately beautiful and charming than the original. What such gardens could look like may be seen and admired from Charles Barry's terrace at Harewood, which overlooks a broad expanse of gently rising, undulating countryside. A harmonious juxtaposition of swathes of woodland, open spaces and clumps of trees stretches away to the horizon. In the foreground, the immensity of the sky is reflected in a (man-made) lake. In 1758, the year when work began on RIEVAULX TERRACE, and again in 1781, Harewood benefited from the services of Lancelot 'Capability' Brown, still the best-known eighteenth-century landscape gardener, who carried the programme whereby gardens imitated Nature to an unsurpassed acme of perfection. Our journey through the history of the English garden culminates in the great gardens in the South of England.

A

DESCRIPTION

O F

HAWKSTONE,

The SEAT of

Sir RICHARD HILL, Bart.

ONE OF THE

Knights of the Shire for the County

of SALOP.

By T. RODENHURST.

The SECOND EDITION,

With feveral ALTERATIONS and ADDITIONS

Where Nature paints, what beauties fill the mind!
And how the foul expands with joys refin'd!
Reflection feizes, and to man difplays
Infinite Wifdom—claiming all our Praife.
PROSPECT, A POEM, BY E. T.

SHREWSBURY:

Printed and Sold by T. WOOD, Bookfeller.

Sold alfo by G. ROBINSON, No. 25, Pater Nofter-Row, and
J. WALTER, Charing-Crofs, LONDON.

M,DCC,LXXXIV.

Title page of Thomas Rodenhurst's guide to
the garden of Hawkstone (1781)

A steady foot and a steady head, or
excursions to the Alps and Tahiti

Hawkstone Park, Shropshire

Anyone returning from yorkshire to the South of England would find a detour to Hawkstone Park well worthwhile. This was where, at great expense and employing many original ideas, Sir Rowland Hill (1705–83) and his son Richard (1732–1809) transformed Shropshire's hilly landscape into a highly individual natural spectacle for which the word 'garden' seems scarcely appropriate. In its day, Hawkstone was an indispensable port of call on the English garden tour. The property was split up and some of it sold off in the nineteenth century. The general public did not regain access to the surviving core of the estate – the area to which it owes its reputation – until 1993.

Four sandstone hills – ELYSIAN HILL, TERRACE HILL, RED CASTLE HILL and GROTTO HILL – form the nucleus of the park, which is reminiscent less of the mellow landscape of northern Italy than of rugged, rocky Alpine scenery. Crossing the Alps was an obligatory part of the Grand Tour. Anyone wishing to visit the plains of Lombardy, the Veneto or the Campagna had first to negotiate one of the inhospitable Alpine passes, which in those days were not without their dangers. In so doing, south-bound travellers found that even this type of scenery, hitherto considered

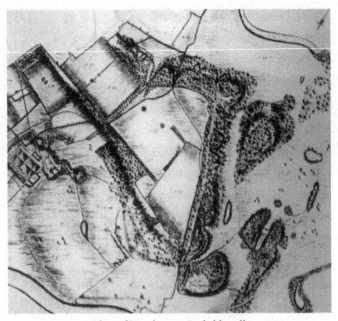

Plan of Hawkstone Park (detail)

hostile, ugly and dangerous, had its charms; sheer rock faces
and ravines looked threatening, but that their very air of
menace lent the scenery a special excitement – provided,
of course, that you yourself were safe from harm. Grand
Tourists in transit through the Alps discovered the sublimity of Nature and the charms of a landscape that was wild,
pristine and rugged as opposed to even and beautiful in an
obvious way. Countless travel books, letters and diaries told
of breathtaking vistas, eternal ice, and the unbridled power
of thundering waterfalls. Paintings and engravings popu-
larized representations of correspondingly dramatic natural
spectacles. (The Italian landscape painter Salvator Rosa,

nicknamed 'wild Salvator', was particularly noted for his depictions of 'sublime' scenery.) More and more people ventured into the mountains to see the sublime with their own eyes. By the end of the century, Switzerland had overtaken Italy and become the most-visited country in Europe – the first to be developed for tourism on account of its scenic attractions.

The Urn

In addition to reminiscences of Italy and the celebration of natural beauty, landscape gardens began to convey references to the Alps and delight in their romantic desolation, effectively emphasizing these with the aid of dilapidated Gothic walls, ruined 'devil's bridges' and gloomy grottoes. Of all representations of the sublimity of Nature in gardens of the eighteenth century, Hawkstone is the most spectacular.

Today, visitors enter the park by way of the former greenhouse on ELYSIAN HILL, which adjoins TERRACE HILL. Over three-quarters of a mile in extent, the latter affords views of the valleys winding between the sandstone hills and of the surrounding countryside. In its thirteenth-century RED CASTLE, Hawkstone Park also possesses the ruins of a genuine medieval castle perfectly in keeping with the rocky landscape. But the true sensation is GROTTO HILL, which the Hills crowned with an imitation of a 'ruined' Gothic arch. Narrow paths wind their way up the hill. Cut into the steep, reddish rock, they lead to all manner of follies and vantage points, for instance to a Gothic tower, a monument with a viewing platform, and an urn whose plinth records a dramatic incident that once occurred there. In dramatizing the landscape, the Hills often made use of the contemporary technique whereby visitors to gardens were coaxed into a certain mood and had their imagination stimulated by means of inscriptions and notice boards.

Hermitages were a popular feature in gardens that aimed at 'the sublime', because they were a reminder of life close to Nature in times of yore. Confronted by such caves or holes in the ground, visitors could picture how people might have lived before the advent of civilization and progress, enlightenment, and material prosperity. The hermitage at Hawkstone was actually inhabited by a genuine hermit whom the Hills employed to occupy their folly. Francis by name, he was under orders to recite a saying whenever visitors passed by. This surprise effect, which startled elegant gentlemen and sensitive ladies on their walks, was far from unique to Hawkstone. Charles Hamilton, for example, placed a newspaper advertisement for a suitable hermit for Painshill Park, his estate at Cobham. The applicant was forbidden to cut his hair, beard or nails, was not permitted to leave the grounds or utter a word, and would not be paid until he had conscientiously fulfilled his terms of employment for a period of seven years. The hermit at Hawkstone was replaced in the nineteenth century by an automaton. Today, he addresses visitors by way of a video installation.

Hawkstone's greatest attraction is a cave system inside GROTTO HILL. Modern visitors can hire pocket lamps, whose use is 'highly recommended' by a notice board at the entrance to the park. This advice should be taken seriously, for the route through Hawkstone Park keeps disappearing into subterranean catacombs of indeterminate extent, and their twists and turns can envelop one in total darkness. These passages lead to chambers hewn out of the rock or apertures revealing dramatic views of ravines and precipitous slopes. An eighteenth-century guide designed to attract visitors, which was even sold in London, contributed to the park's reputation. Describing the grotto, it declared that the whole thing had been boldly and

Rocky chamber inside GROTTO HILL

skillfully executed in perfect keeping with the surrounding scenery. There was none of the usual small-scale 'prettiness' that tended to turn grottoes into artificial 'baby houses' rather than big, natural, romantic caverns.

The pleasurable thrill inspired by sublime natural scenery was stage-managed with particular skill at the grotto exits. Scarcely have visitors emerged into daylight after a long spell in darkness when the path suddenly descends a rocky ledge with a deep gorge yawning beneath it. Since 1774, the most impressive of these spots has been known as THE AWFUL PRECIPICE, after the startled cry uttered by one of Hawkstone's most celebrated visitors, the indefatigable scholar and essayist Dr Johnson. In an exhaustive account of the impression Hawkstone had made on him, he stated that those who climbed its crags wondered how they had got there and doubted whether they would ever find their way back. Walking the park was an adventure, he wrote, and leaving it an escape.

Contemporary descriptions of Hawkstone Park read like accounts of journeys through the Alps. Since people were used to confusing artificial landscapes with the originals in their imagination, literary recapitulations of their experiences in the park effaced the distinction between original and copy, which is the first thing that strikes the modern visitor. A signpost on GROTTO HILL prescribed what form of experience should be undergone there: 'To a Scene in Switzerland,' it announced. With all due respect to Shropshire's unusual rock formations, the said comparison required a considerable stretch of the imagination. This was promoted not only by the signpost but also by the construction of a narrow, makeshift-looking bridge of undressed tree trunks, which conveyed the impression that, had it not been thrown across a deep ravine, further progress would have been impossible. The contemporary Hawkstone guide warned: 'For the enjoyment of this charming and astonishing scene, a steady head and a steady foot are both equally necessary.'

But the Hills did not confine themselves to staging an alpine mountainscape in their rocky park: they also wanted to transport those left at home to other regions of the world described by travellers. Tahiti and other South Sea islands aroused great interest during the latter decades of the eighteenth century, particularly after the publication of Captain Cook's account of his first voyage there. An engraving from Cook's journals provided the reference for a straw hut in Hawkstone's mountainous park. It was heralded by a signpost reading: 'To a Scene of Otaheite.'

Stowe: TEMPLE OF CONCORD AND VICTORY,
GRECIAN VALLEY and Greville Column
(engraving by Bickham after Chatelain, 1753)

*Freedom, Elysium and satire, or 'the
best ideas of Paradise that can be'*

Stowe, Buckinghamshire

In 1731 the poet Alexander Pope had composed a long
encomium on the garden at Chiswick entitled *Epistle to
Lord Burlington*. This outlined the fundamental characteristics of landscape gardening and archetype of an English
garden, which was initially intended to reflect a just political constitution and a good social order. Natural freedom
and constitutional liberty became synonymous in the
English garden's iconography. Pope himself had called for
the adaptation of gardens to their untouched natural surroundings, and his words were often quoted:

> 'Consult the Genius of the Place in all; / That tells the
> Waters or to rise, or fall, [...] / Calls in the Country,
> catches opening glades, / Joins willing woods, and varies
> shades from shades [...] / Nature shall join you, Time shall
> make it grow / A Work to wonder at – perhaps a STOW.'

Stowe was Pope's favourite garden. Referring to the
Temple family's country estate, one of the most important contributions to the development of garden design in
England, he declared that, if any place this side of paradise
could raise him above all earthly things, it would be Stowe.

Over a period of decades, the spacious Baroque park that had once attracted visitors developed into one of the largest, loveliest and most impressive gardens in the English style. Every phase in the development of eighteenth-century garden design has left traces there. Stow possesses long driveways like Castle Howard and the political programme of Chiswick; temples in the Greek, Palladian and Gothic styles; an ingenious system of serpentine paths and planting effects; and a network of visual axes designed to create relationships between different views, the whole thing being enclosed by one of the longest and oldest ha-has in England. Still visible in front of the south face of the majestic house (now the home of a famous public school) are the remains of the original Baroque garden, although the regular parterre was ploughed up in the 1740s and replaced by a broad expanse of lawn. The elongated artificial lake, with its irregular, seemingly natural shoreline, still bears the name OCTAGON LAKE after its original shape.

All the leading eighteenth-century landscape gardeners worked at Stowe. William Kent came there from nearby Rousham before taking over the design of its garden entirely. His successor was the man destined to bring the imitation of Nature in a garden to absolute perfection: Lancelot 'Capability' Brown (1716–83). He was the first landscape gardener never to have practised another profession. Employed at Stowe from 1740 onwards, he was promoted after Kent's death in 1748 to be head gardener in charge of a staff of thirty. In 1751 he left Stowe and went free-lance, his services becoming more and more sought-after by owners of gardens throughout the country.

Instead of building over his predecessors' work at Stowe, Brown continued it and welded the various parts of the garden into a whole. It takes time to tour the grounds. A full circuit is all of three miles long, and even that excludes a number of bypaths. An inventory made in 1990, in the course of extensive restoration work, identified more than ninety separate scenes of varying elaboration. Many garden buildings have disappeared, but over three dozen are still standing (or have been restored). In conformity with the dimensions of the site, many of these structures are exceptionally big. The Temples were a wealthy family, and Sir Richard Temple, later 1st Viscount Cobham (1675–1749), and his nephew Richard Grenville, 2nd Earl Temple (1711–79), invested a great deal of money in their garden, whose fame soon spread far beyond the shores of England. Stowe boasted the first garden guide ever printed (in 1742), and its park played an important part in popularizing the fashion for English gardens on the Continent. What Versailles was to the French garden, Stowe soon became for the English.

Sir Richard Temple, 4th baronet and Viscount Cobham from 1718 onwards, was a friend not only of Alexander Pope but also of John Vanbrugh, who designed several temples and garden scenes for Stowe when the grounds began to be enlarged in 1715. William Kent broke up their formal arrangement and Lancelot Brown eventually exposed them entirely to the interplay of the boundary between Nature and Art. In Temple's earliest designs, however, the imitation of Nature was outweighed by the politico-philosophical programme. Not until Kent arrived on the scene did garden designers develop a Nature-oriented formal language that subtly presented an alternative to the formal parks of France by transposing the concept of political freedom – and, with it, a critique of absolutism – into the ideal of a seemingly natural and freely unfolding garden landscape.

Earlier on, the garden designers of Lord Burlington, Henry Hoare and Richard Temple had relied mainly on buildings and sculptures to signal that a new age had dawned when the Stuart regime was overthrown in 1688. This harking back to the buildings of antiquity, and, before long, to those of the Renaissance and Gothic periods (the most important historical epochs antedating the age of absolutism), served to demonstrate the new spirit that was to permeate the 'Augustan Age'.

No English garden is as dominated by its political programme as Stowe, but its significance underwent a shift. When Temple began to redesign it, he belonged to the circle of leading Whigs. Like Lord Burlington's, however, his political career ended in 1733, after disagreements with the chancellor, Robert Walpole. Now Viscount Cobham, Temple joined other Whigs who preferred to go into opposition. Stowe became a meeting place for all who remained faithful to the Whigs' original programme and opposed the corruption, intrigues and nepotism rife in London. What had at first been planned as a general, philosophical outline became a political manifesto espoused by the opposition. The earnestness with which Lord Cobham pursued this concern was admired but also derided. It is quite possible, though not proven, that West Wykeham's cheerfully ironical garden programme was also intended as a riposte to Stowe.

Temple's idea for his philosophical garden was probably

inspired by Joseph Addison's essay in the *Spectator* of 21 January 1710. In this, Addison recounts an allegorical dream which begins in a forest full of people. In their company he proceeds along a path that leads past a series of buildings including a Temple of the Virtues, a Temple of Honour, and a ruined Temple of Vanity. All these buildings can be found at Stowe, where the links between the English garden and literature have seldom been more clearly demonstrated. In reviving the civilization of ancient Rome, 'Augustan' England had also resurrected literary satire in the Juvenal tradition. Pope, Addison, Swift and many other authors of this period used satire as a means of exposing their opponents and depicting their own ideals. The garden at Stowe, which was intended to demonstrate the utopia of a better world, is also pervaded by the spirit of literary satire. To quote Elizabeth Montague's enthusiastic tribute in 1744: 'Stowe is beyond description, it gives the best ideas of paradise than can be.'

Visitors are confronted, right at the beginning of their tour, by what is now Stowe's most massive building, one of the biggest temples ever erected in an English garden: the TEMPLE OF CONCORD AND VICTORY. The lofty, colonnaded front faces west, so the columns take on a reddish tinge at sunset. The landscape gardeners of the eighteenth century, in designing their artificial paradises, did not leave the interplay of light and shade to chance, nor even to the trees' various shades of green and the autumnal colouring of their foliage. This temple, whose tympanum is populated by all manner of exotic creatures (including a turtle), is not modeled on any existing building. Work on it began

The Gothic Temple.

in 1747, and it was subsequently dedicated to the victorious alliance between England and Prussia in the Seven Years' War. Stretching away from its steps is the GRECIAN VALLEY, a long, grassy depression excavated between 1747 and 1749 by Lancelot Brown, who originally intended it to be an artificial lake. The GRECIAN VALLEY provides a foretaste of the later style of Brown's gardens, which make use of basic natural elements: lawns, water, trees, sky, and light. The dimensions of the temple and the scale of the valley far exceed the landscaping and architectural allusions of most English gardens. Brown's gardens make fewer demands on the visitor's imagination than earlier landscape gardens. He had no wish to conjure up an ideal landscape; he aimed to create one, and at Stowe he began to do this.

On the left, as one walks along the edge of the valley, the garden opens out into the surrounding area beyond the ha-ha. The path skirts various buildings and enters a wood. In a clearing there, mounted on deliberately unadorned plinths, are seven strange figures. These are Sunna, Mona, Tiw, Woden, Thuner, Friga and Saetern, the Germanic deities that have lent their names to the days of the week (in English as well as German). These SAXON DEITIES were intended as a reminder that it was Saxons who once introduced another and better social order into the British Isles. At the same time, Lord Cobham may have meant to suggest that Britain's newly acquired freedom was underwritten by the house of Hanover. There is scarcely one feature of the gardens at Stowe that fails to transmit a topical message. This also applies to the GOTHIC TEMPLE of 1744. Half tower, half Gothic church, it stands some distance away on a hill surrounded by free-standing, unpruned trees. An inscription on this Gothic building, with its crenellations, turrets and pointed-arched windows, proclaims: 'To the Liberties of our Ancestors'. Like the Gothic tower at Stourhead, which originated twenty years later, it commemorates the legendary King Alfred. Put into the right frame of mind by these allusions to the British Isles' long tradition of liberty and justice, one enters the heart of the gardens, the ELYSIAN FIELDS. This picturesque valley with a little river winding along it is the work of William Kent, and was nearing completion when Brown came to Stowe in 1740. As at Chiswick and Rousham, Kent made the river issue from a cascade in a grotto. Known as the STYX, it separates us from the Elysian Fields, the ancient Greeks' paradise and meeting

The Temple of Antient Virtue.

place of heroes whom the gods have selected for immortality. This valley was where Cobham, with Kent's assistance, made Joseph Addison's allegorical dream come true.

The circular temple on a hill overlooking the STYX bears the name TEMPLE OF ANCIENT VIRTUE, as the inscription above the entrance – 'Priscae Virtuti' – indicates. Within it are statues of Homer, Epaminondas, Socrates and Lycurgus: the greatest poet, the most important philosopher, the bravest warrior of the ancient world, and the initiator of a new legal code which bestowed a liberal constitution on his country, Sparta (as the Whigs had done in England). It is the Temple of the Virtues from Addison's literary dream. In its immediate vicinity stands his Temple of Vanity, the badly dilapidated ruin of a classical temple known as the TEMPLE OF MODERN VIRTUE. Its ruined walls used to house a headless figure in contemporary dress,

The Palladian Bridge.

by which was undoubtedly meant the times in general and, possibly, Sir Robert Walpole in particular. The lawn around the TEMPLE OF ANCIENT VIRTUE was always kept short, whereas the ruined TEMPLE OF MODERN VIRTUE was surrounded by a neglected, overgrown field (until it completely disappeared at some stage).

In Kent's ELYSIAN FIELDS, the Temple of Honour in Addison's dream took the form of the TEMPLE OF BRITISH WORTHIES. It stands on the other side of the STYX and displays Palladian features, so it embodies a contemporary adaptation of the Graeco-Roman culture then considered exemplary. A marble statue of Mercury, the messenger of the gods, one of whose duties was to conduct future immortals to Elysium, indicates that this is where candidates for a place of honour in paradise are assembled. Gazing across the STYX at the TEMPLE OF ANCIENT VIRTUE are sixteen stone busts of meritorious individuals including Alexander Pope, Inigo Jones, John Milton, King Alfred, William

Shakespeare, John Locke, Isaac Newton, Francis Drake, and – the only woman – Queen Elizabeth I. A sixteenth 'British worthy' is accorded an inscription on the back. This states that it commemorates 'Signor Fido', an Italian of good family who came to England not to bite its inhabitants, like most of his compatriots, but to lead an honourable life. The lengthy eulogy ends by assuring the reader that 'this stone' is devoid of flattery, being dedicated to a greyhound, not a man.

Only one contemporary had already gained access to Elysium: Captain Thomas Grenville, one of the childless Cobham's numerous nephews, who was mortally wounded in a naval engagement against the French in 1747. In his memory Cobham erected a column, which was transferred to the ELYSIAN FIELDS in 1756. Since then, the tip of the column has been occupied by Calliope, the muse of heroic literature, instead of Neptune.

One leaves the ELYSIAN FIELDS by descending a grassy slope to the lake, which at this point is as narrow as a river, and reaches the area of garden on the other side by way of an elegant covered bridge. Constructed in 1737, it is called the PALLADIAN BRIDGE, although no such design by Palladio is known. It is more likely to be a copy of an almost identical bridge erected a year earlier in the grounds of Wilton House near Salisbury. Another copy was built in 1755 at Prior Park, near Bath. Landscape gardeners sought inspiration from other parks, not solely in distant lands and architectural reference books, so garden tourists of the eighteenth century were accustomed to encountering more than one building of the same design.

The most important edifices on the south shore of the lake are a TEMPLE OF VENUS, a hermitage by Kent, and the TEMPLE OF FRIENDSHIP. This was where Cobham consorted with his political allies, hence the existence in the basement of a kitchen and a well-stocked wine cellar. The Whigs who had gone into opposition in 1733 became known as 'Boy Patriots' or 'Cobham's Cubs' (they included several of Cobham's nephews). They supported Frederick, Prince of Wales, in his dispute with George II. Frederick was entertained at Stowe in 1737, and the TEMPLE OF FRIENDSHIP was built to commemorate his visit. Its position enabled Cobham to look out over his gardens.

The panoramic view across the lake and the PALLADIAN BRIDGE is bounded by belts of trees. THE TEMPLE OF VENUS, the TEMPLE OF ANCIENT VIRTUE and the GOTHIC TEMPLE can be seen from here, as can a brightly painted CHINESE HOUSE in a small clearing and a free-standing triumphal arch in a spacious meadow. This forms the entrance to the western part of the garden, whose theme is love, not politics. The central and longest line of sight from the TEMPLE OF FRIENDSHIP is focused on the classicistic QUEEN'S TEMPLE, where Lady Cobham used to gather her friends around her while the menfolk talked politics in the TEMPLE OF FRIENDSHIP.

The magnificent prospect that unfolds between the garden's east and west sections has inherited its original Baroque central axis. One looks far out into the countryside across a broad expanse of lawn, the lake and the ha-ha. In the middle of the fringe of trees on the skyline is a triumphal arch through which the eye seems to gaze into infinity. Presenting a seemingly untouched immensity of ideal landscape devoid of boundaries became the programme espoused by Lancelot Brown, who created this vista.

Blenheim. View of the palace from the north
(Engraving by John Boydell, 1752)

The riverless bridge, or a contest
between gigantomaniacs

Blenheim, Oxfordshire

' Thames, thames, you will never forgive me,' Lancelot Brown exclaimed after excavating two huge,
interconnected lakes in Blenheim Park, which he evi-
dently considered more beautiful than all the landscape
scenes produced by Nature itself, the banks of the proud
Thames included. Even King George III declared: 'We have
nothing to compare with this!'

There are two entrances to the park and gardens at Blenheim. The very distance between them already suggests that
the lofty perimeter wall conceals a property of vast dimensions: some 2000 acres of landscaped grounds. Visitors
should definitely use the rear entrance, where a road on the
edge of the small village of Woodstock ends in front of a
high, narrow triumphal arch in the Roman style. The view
that unfolds beyond this gate surpasses all expectations: a
handsome lake and wooded island in a dip surrounded by
rolling, grassy hills and scattered clumps of trees. It would
hardly occur to anyone unaware of being in a garden that
the whole thing is the product of art, not Nature. All that
might arouse the beholder's suspicions is the harmony of
the scene and the perfect interrelationship of its constituent parts. Nature, as we conceive of it, does not in general

look like this. Although the shapes are easy on the eye, the immense extent of this landscape and the dimensions of the buildings that go with it are positively breathtaking. The lake is spanned by a massive bridge, and looming in the distance are the sand-coloured walls of a palace that looks as if it is out of this world. Putting this view into words has surpassed garden tourists' rhetoric for two hundred years. One of them described entering by way of the triumphal arch as follows: 'It is the transition not from nothing to something, but from nothing to everything.'

As a freelance landscape gardener, Lancelot Brown developed his experiment at Stowe into an unmistakable style of his own. His gardens can, at a pinch, be mistaken for Nature itself. He did not content himself with allusions and miniature imitations; his landscapes were truly intended to be a match for Nature. He wanted to consummate the possibilities inherent in Creation. He had never been to Italy; his ideal of landscape was moulded from the first by working in a garden. Instead of horticulturally transposing Claude Lorrain's pictures and descriptions of landscapes by visitors to Italy, he looked at the green hills of England with Lorrain's eyes and sought to prove that it was possible to lend them, too, the harmonious beauty for which Italian landscape paintings were so admired, and which lived on in Grand Tourists' recollections of the rolling hills of the Campagna. Brown's ideas worked particularly well when money was no object and he had unlimited space to work with. Blenheim presented him with a special challenge. He had not only to remodel the landscape, but to contend with the legacy of an artist who had striven, in his own way, to break with convention half a century earlier: the buildings Brown had to integrate into his landscape had been designed by John Vanbrugh.

On 13 August 1704, allied troops under the command of John Churchill, 1st Duke of Marlborough, defeated Louis XIV's army at the battle of Blenheim, a village on the Danube. Queen Anne, who had ruled England since 1702, expressed her gratitude by presenting him with the royal hunting lodge and estate at Woodstock and promising to build him a country house there, to be called Blenheim in memory of his victory. No one seemed better suited to building such a temple of fame than John Vanbrugh, who had already demonstrated at Castle Howard that he knew how to build on a grand scale. The former playwright and scenic artist designed a palace that need not fear comparison with Castle Howard, relying even more heavily there on theatrical effects. With an eye to its perspectival effect, the interlocking three-wing layout is conceived in accordance with the rules of stage design. When seen from the garden side the building narrows; it positively sucks up space. Differing in height and ornamented in a variety of ways, the turrets, chimneys and roofs do not relieve its bombastic appearance; instead, they intensify its playful and, at the same time, massive monumentality. Visitors who slowly approach the palace, perhaps at twilight or when swaths of mist are drifting across the grounds, will readily feel they are succumbing to a mirage.

Blenheim Palace is regarded as the acme of English Baroque. Its Baroque delight in pomp, in the displaying of power and wealth, is coupled here with Vanbrugh's

Blenheim. Palace and bridge (engraving of 1787)

theatrical gigantomania. The house is big, but its wings and colonnades and eaves of differing height make it look much bigger. 'Behold the glorious piles ascending, / Columns swelling, arches bending,' wrote Joseph Addison. As at Castle Howard, so, at Blenheim, Nicholas Hawksmoor helped to put Vanbrugh's plans into effect. Here too, the heart of the building is a huge hall over twenty metres high, and here too Vanbrugh naturally insisted on an immensely long drive by way of which visitors would approach his palace by degrees. However, its siting was so impractical that it was very seldom used.

Vanbrugh wanted Blenheim to compete with Versailles, the celebrated palace of the defeated French king. As early as 1705, work commenced on an immense parterre running along the north front. This was nearly 800 metres in length.

Vanbrugh had it enclosed by a stout wall, wide enough to walk along and punctuated by eight massive towers – an impregnable bastion. His task, after all, was to immortalize a military hero and a victorious battle, and Castle Howard had already demonstrated his weakness for the building of fortifications. Much to her annoyance, he even built a huge wall to enclose the flower garden he laid out for Lady Sarah Marlborough.

Vanbrugh's plans were a growing thorn in the duchess's side. She protested vigorously when he wanted to make the medieval remains of Woodstock Manor the focus of a visual axis. Vanbrugh declared that the the finest landscape painters could not have devised a more appropriate scene, but he remained alone in that opinion. It would be another few decades before ruins became a universally popular accessory of landscape compositions, in gardens as well as paintings, and Woodstock Manor had been demolished by then. In the summer of 1716, Vanbrugh finally broke with the duchess and stormed off in a huff. When he paid a last visit to Woodstock in 1725, a year before his death, he was turned away at the gate.

The chief bone of contention between the duchess and the architect she disliked so much was the bridge in the park – 'that damn'd bridge', as Lady Sarah called it. On his plans it bore the proud name PONS BLENHEIMENSIS. Vanbrugh meant it as a reminder that victorious Roman legions had once marched there. He wanted to extend the park's central axis northwards across the bridge, which was to take the form of a Roman viaduct, and along a small valley carved out of the landscape by the little river Glyme.

Vanbrugh's design for the PONS BLENHEIMENSIS

The PONS BLENHEIMENSIS, on which work began in 1708, was intended to be the finest, most magnificent bridge in Europe. Had the arcaded superstructure in the original plans been built, it would have stood twenty-four metres high and contained over thirty rooms. Vanbrugh predicted that Lady Sarah would want to move into his bridge once it was completed. Instead of that, she prevented the second storey from being built.

The real problem was the river Glyme, a small stream barely two or three metres in width. Since it flowed through the central arch of the bridge, which was over thirty metres wide, it must have looked thoroughly grotesque. From the sublime to the ridiculous is but a short step. During the 1720s Lady Sarah tried to widen the river, at least to some extent, by canalizing it. However, that was no match for

Vanbrugh's bridge. The fact that a great deal of money (£20,000) had been spent on building a huge bridge and another vast sum invested to ensure that some water flowed through it did nothing to quell the ridicule levelled at this absurd situation. It was half a century before the bridge got the water its size merited.

In 1763 George Spencer, 4th Duke of Marlborough, employed Lancelot Brown to convert his formal park into a landscape garden. Brown's ten-year stint at Blenheim made him famous. Even today, he is still the only landscape gardener known to the general public. He earned his nickname, 'Capability Brown', from the fact that he always began by assessing a property's 'capabilities', or potential for improvement. For that was Brown's programme: to make it as beautiful as its potential (and his employer's financial means) allowed. He wanted to assuage the yearning for an ideal image of Nature, which had been fostered as much by enthusiasm for landscape painting as by the landscape quotations in English gardens. This he did by evoking the beauty of Nature not only by means of quotations and copies, but by the creation of truly perfect landscapes out of what was already there.

The scale at Blenheim was prescribed by its buildings: the gigantic palace, the huge bridge, the triumphal arch Lady Sarah employed Hawksmoor to erect in 1723, in memory of her late husband, and a forty-metre Column of Victory erected around 1730 as the culmination of the parterre's central axis. Brown assigned these buildings, which had dominated the old park, an appropriate place in the landscape. He began by ploughing up Vanbrugh's parterre and demolishing all the walls. All that eventually survived of the formal gardens was Vanbrugh's kitchen garden and the GRAND AVENUE, which extends northwards for three miles beyond the Column of Victory. Formal parterres were not relaid around the house until the twentieth century.

Brown's greatest challenge was to integrate Vanbrugh's bridge in the landscape and create the impression that its construction was a natural necessity. To this end he dammed the river, thereby flooding the bridge's lower rooms and making it look lower than Vanbrugh had intended. On either side of the bridge he created lakes out of the pent-up water and remodeled their banks until they met with his approval. The dam he transformed into a cascade. Here, the waters of the Glyme gush over a picturesque slab of rock that looks as if it has always been there, creating a scene that Salvator Rosa might have painted. The 4th duke contrived to dramatize this effect by installing a path above the waterfall. The sound of rushing water grew steadily louder and more insistent as Marlborough's guests neared the cascade. That sound alone was enough to conjure up visions of a 'sublime' garden in their imagination, though nothing of the kind could be seen far and wide. All at once, however, they found a boulder barring their path. By releasing a hidden spring, Marlborough could suddenly transform their disappointment into boundless admiration: the rock rolled aside to reveal a view of the cascade.

Brown concealed the boundaries of his gardens either by means of ha-has or, as here at Blenheim, by hiding walls behind belts of trees. At Chiswick Lord Burlington had incised lanes and clearings into a wood to create his garden space. Brown's gardens, by contrast, are open landscapes structured with the aid of expanses of water, grassy hills and clumps of trees. The entire area is composed to form a totality, not just individual scenes. Brown disclosed some views and concealed others by skillfully raising and lowering the terrain. All his views are the product of careful calculation, even though such calculation is imperceptible. No plan, painting or photograph can reproduce his dynamic treatment of space. Rhythmically structured landscape formations are set in motion as we traverse that space, creating a series of new vistas and impressions. Carefully sited clumps of trees play an important part in this process because they help to structure the terrain and guide the eye. They look a trifle too neat to seem truly natural, but that very fact promotes the impression of an ideal landscape in an almost imperceptible manner. The sparsely wooded countryside picks up the rhythmical interplay of these clumps beyond the borders of the park. Thus, Brown's seemingly restrained but elaborate manipulation of the landscape extends as far as the horizon, and our imagination automatically extends it still further. The garden no longer quotes the beauties of the world; the whole world becomes an English garden.

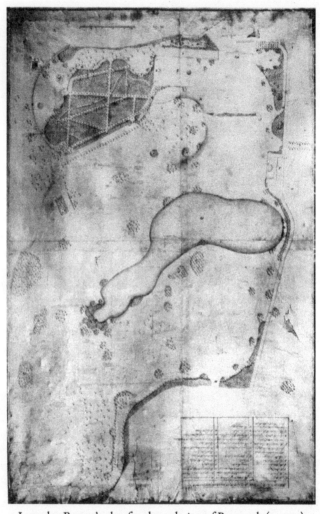

Lancelot Brown's plan for the redesign of Petworth (c. 1753)

Lady Nature's second husband, or a walk into infinity

Petworth, Sussex

L ancelot brown, the former gardener's boy, rose within a very short time to become a celebrated landscape gardener and was soon receiving one commission after another. Appointed 'Royal Gardener at Hampton Court and Richmond' in 1764, he was forever on the move and engaged on several sites concurrently. His oeuvre embraces over 200 gardens. Bit by bit, with the enthusiasm of a perfectionist, he adapted the English landscape to the ideal he had formed of it. He declined an offer from Scotland on the grounds that he still hadn't finished with England. Horace Walpole called him 'Lady Nature's second Husband'.

One of the first jobs Brown undertook from Stowe was the redesign of Petworth Park in Sussex. He was able to realize his idea of a beautified landscape more freely there than anywhere else. He may have created more beautiful gardens (probably his finest man-made landscape is that of Bowood in Wiltshire), and Blenheim's huge buildings may be more spectacular, but no English garden conveys his brilliant treatment of landscape more impressively than the 700-acre park he created for Charles Wyndham, 2nd Earl of Egremont, at Petworth from 1751 onwards.

Charles Wyndham had also been on the Grand Tour before he acquired Petworth by marriage in 1750, a seventeenth-century building with the customary French parterre. As early as 1751, Brown was invited to make suggestions as to how the park could be redesigned. His first planting plan, which shows a huge tract of land with a multitude of trees scattered across it seemingly at random, some on their own, others in clumps, betrays none of the impressions a visit to the park has in store.

Petworth would be worth a visit even without its park. Charles Wyndham had returned from his Grand Tour with numerous paintings, mainly landscapes, and he also belonged to a circle of English art lovers, which was then discovering the Dutch painters of the seventeenth century. Wyndham laid the foundations of a choice art collection, which his son built up into one of the finest in the country. Hundreds of paintings are hanging in Petworth House cheek by jowl, among them works by Reynolds, Gainsborough, van Dyck, Titian, Rubens, Füssli, Hieronymus Bosch and Rogier van der Weyden. It also contains the largest private collection of oils by William Turner. In the 1820s a picture gallery was added on the north side of the house. Rows of paintings cover its walls from floor to ceiling, and statues and other sculptures are distributed around the room. Visiting this gallery is a memorable experience, especially on fine days, when the pale marble sculptures and the paintings on its dark red walls are bathed in the sunbeams streaming down through the skylights. Also represented in the collection, needless to say, are painters whose pictures helped to shape the contemporary ideal of landscape: Gaspard Daughet (who adopted the surname of his famous brother-in-law, Nicholas Poussin), Jacob van

Ruisdael, and, of course, Claude Lorrain. The windows of the drawing room on the ground floor of Petworth House enable one to see how Lancelot Brown adapted Nature to the atmospheric landscape ideal that underlies those paintings. They also disclose an astonishing fact: although apparently haphazard, the huge park's scattered clumps of trees are disposed in such a way that each window affords a long and unobstructed view of the landscape.

Brown's invariable mode of procedure was surprisingly simple and never less than effective: he dammed the stream or river that flowed through a park, however small in volume, thereby creating a lake whose shores he shaped in accordance with the size of the property and his employer's personal taste and financial resources. Then he modeled the terrain itself. None of the constituent features that governed so many of Brown's gardens – lakes, grassy hills, clumps of trees, ha-has – was new, but his drastic reduction of garden design to those few elements produced remarkable effects again and again. Brown's theme was not antiquity or the Italian landscape; he was interested in staging spectacular demonstrations of the way in which we experience Nature as the space that surrounds us. In so doing, he largely effaced the boundary between art and Nature. Brown often made a point of separating the markedly artificial from the seemingly natural parts of a garden – a separation destined to become an established feature of the great nineteenth-century garden designs (and also of the celebrated parks landscaped by Peter Joseph Lenné and Prince Pückler in Germany).

The thirty-acre Pleasure Ground on the north side of the

house is the only part of the garden at Petworth to which Brown did not make substantial changes. The old structures were retained, although he planted a large number of trees and shrubs, laid serpentine paths, and erected two classical temples there. The Pleasure Ground was badly affected in 1987, when a storm ravaged Petworth and felled 600 trees. However, a costly planting programme is ensuring that the original appearance of the place will be restored.

The park is enclosed by a long wall, not that any of it is visible from within. In some places the soil has been heaped up level with the top of the wall, turning it into a ha-ha. Elsewhere, a belt of trees on the edge of the park ensures that one would never at any point suspect that one was in an enclosed area. The Pleasure Ground is also separated from the park by a ha-ha. That became necessary mainly because it is inhabited by a herd of rare deer. The animals, which probably hail from Eastern Europe, were imported in the middle of the eighteenth century, when it was fashionable to keep exotic game in gardens. A herd of two thousand deer is said to have grazed at Blenheim. Petworth still has over a thousand today. They make a picturesque sight as they gallop between the clumps of trees and across the hills or stand grazing beside the lake.

Brown converted the formal parterre flanking the west side of the house into a broad expanse of lawn. Reaching far out into the grounds, this is surrounded by an open stretch of landscape whose alternation of pale green fields and dark islands of trees extends beyond the wall and as far as the skyline. In the foreground, the lake threads its way through this serene and splendid scene like a gleaming ribbon. It is

William Turner: Petworth Park (1827–8)

as if Claude Lorrain had painted the world not as he wished it to be, but as it really is. The landscape seems interminable, even when we slowly begin to traverse it. Walkers move freely throughout its extent, their eyes and footsteps guided by the hills, valleys, lake and clumps of trees. These ensure that the landscape is constantly changing. On the right is a hill with a grassy valley beyond it; on the left, open countryside. Beyond each hill lie more hills. It is the landscape itself that gently compels us to take certain routes and seek out certain views.

The lake, which seems to increase in size with every step we take, is probably the loveliest of Brown's innumerable garden lakes. He excavated 47,000 tons of soil, and 17,000 tons of clay had to be spread over the sandy ground in order to retain the water in the basin. Brown's lakes invariably look bigger than they are; they also change shape according to our point of view. Like Kent's garden paths, their conformation is determined by a semblance of infinity. Their shorelines suggest that they continue when they do not. We sometimes get the impression that they are two bodies of water, not one, or that we are approaching a river. Even the sky and the light appear to be at the disposal of Lancelot Brown's landscaping. Cloud shadows drift between clumps of trees and grassy valleys change character according to the position of the sun. In the afternoon, when the sun is setting, the clumps of trees cast long shadows. This is a favourite time for the deer to roam across the hills. The park extends for over two miles, but it is less its acreage that conveys an impression of size and extent than its landscaping. Walking through it becomes a walk into infinity.

Instead of presenting a simulacrum of Nature, Brown seems to present us with Nature itself. Therein lies his greatest achievement, but it also formed the basis of certain charges laid against him. His imitation of Nature was so perfect, people wondered why his patrons had to go to such vast expense if all that resulted was a landscape instead of a landscape garden. Indeed, many accused him of destroying beautiful old gardens.

To most people, however, Capability Brown remains the greatest landscape gardener of the eighteenth century. Prince Pückler called him the Shakespeare of garden design, and his admiration for Brown's treatment of space is apparent from his magnificent park at Muskau (where he went to the lengths of diverting the river Neisse because its course was not as he envisioned it). Painters, too, have keenly admired Lancelot Brown's gardens. This is not as self-evident as it may seem. There are not very many paintings of eighteenth-century landscape gardens. The latter, after all, are picturesque interpretations of Nature like the paintings themselves. They are difficult to depict because the difference between Nature and imitation is undetectable, and that tension is just what sustains the design, quotations and allusions of the gardens at Rousham, Stourhead or Stowe. Not until English gardens approximated so closely to Nature that the two could genuinely be confused did they become a landscape painter's motif once more. William Turner, who was a frequent guest at Petworth in the second and third decades of the nineteenth century, painted a whole series of pictures of its garden. Blenheim was another of his motifs. Like Brown and other landscape gardeners, Turner had made a close study of Claude Lorrain's landscape paintings, and he and Lorrain are accorded a small room of their own in London's National Gallery. Turner was also able to employ Brown's beautified landscape as a reference because its size and extent did not restrict the painter's creative scope. Lorrain's view of the world had left its mark on landscape gardens, in which people took an aesthetic view of the beauties of Nature. Towards the end of the eighteenth century artists began to seek these outside gardens as well. Armed with picnic hampers, they took to roaming the countryside in search of natural landscapes worthy of a Claude Lorrain, a Nicholas Poussin, or a Salvator Rosa. It became fashionable to carry a visual aid especially devised for this purpose, which could transform any landscape into a picture of the kind. This was the so-called 'Claude glass', a slightly convex mirror that distorted the scene, lending it the breadth and depth of a seventeenth-century landscape painting.

A new term was coined for those who undertook such excursions: they were christened 'tourists'.

Other landscape gardens in England

AUDLEY END, ESSEX

BOWOOD HOUSE, WILTSHIRE

CHATSWORTH, DERBYSHIRE

CLAREMONT PARK, SURREY

CORSHAM COURT, WILTSHIRE

HAREWOOD HOUSE, YORKSHIRE

HOLKHAM HALL, NORFOLK

HYDE PARK, LONDON

KENSINGTON GARDENS, LONDON

KENWOOD, LONDON

THE LEASOWES, WEST MIDLANDS

LONGLEAT HOUSE, WILTSHIRE

PAINSHILL PARK, SURREY

PRIOR PARK, BATH

RICHMOND PARK, LONDON

ROYAL BOTANIC GARDENS, KEW, LONDON

SEZINCOTE, GLOUCESTERSHIRE

SHEFFIELD PARK, SUSSEX

SHUGBOROUGH HALLL, STAFFORDSHIRE

SYON PARK, LONDON

WARDOUR CASTLE, WILTSHIRE

WILTON HOUSE, WILTSHIRE

WIMPOLE HALL, CAMBRIDGESHIRE

WOBURN ABBEY, BEDFORDSHIRE

WREST PARK, BEDFORDSHIRE

Some English gardens in Germany

BAYREUTH. HERMITAGE AND SANSPAREIL ROCK GARDEN

The Bayreuth Hermitage and the Sanspareil Rock Garden originated before 1750, at a time when the landscape garden had yet to infiltrate the German principalities. Nevertheless, features reminiscent of English gardens can already be found there – a sign that the requirements and sentiments that led to its introduction were already widespread. This applies particularly to Sanspareil, where Margravine Wilhelmine of Bayreuth transformed a romantic, rocky beech grove into a literarily inspired adventure landscape.

WÖRLITZ, NEAR DESSAU

At Wörlitz in 1764, on returning from a visit to England, Prince Leopold Friedrich Franz von Anhalt-Dessau began to create the earliest, most important and arguably most beautiful English garden in Germany. The garden's fame precluded any subsequent alterations. Nowhere else in Germany can the eighteenth-century idea of an English garden be seen in such a complete and pristine state.

DESSAU. GEORGIUM AND LUISIUM

In addition to creating the gardens at Wörlitz, Prince Franz conceived a plan to transform most of his little country into a 'garden realm'. Thus the Georgium at Dessau was also provided with 'English gardens' and the Luisium, a small castle named after the prince's wife, is enclosed by an enchanting little landscape garden.

BURGSTEINFURT. 'BAGNO'
Work began on the 'Bagno' at Burgsteinfurt around 1765. This early amusement park once presented over ninety attractions, most of them copied from other gardens, but very few of these survive. Clustered around its lake are various 'regions' of which one is entitled 'Greece' and another 'Egypt'. The gardens attracted numerous tourists during the eighteenth century.

SCHWETZINGEN
During the 1770s, the landscape gardener Friedrich von Sckell skilfully extended the magnificent Baroque park of Schloss Schwetzingen by adding numerous decorative buildings and 'English' areas notable for their natural scenic beauty. They are still well worth a visit today.

SCHÖNBUSCH, NEAR ASCHAFFENBURG
Around 1775, a small English garden was created here on a peninsula in a bend of the river Main. From 1785 onwards, von Sckell enlarged it into one of the biggest landscape gardens in Germany.

STUTTGART. HOHENHEIM
An exceptionally original English garden took shape at Hohenheim from 1776 onwards. An imitation English

village conveys the impression that it has been erected on the ruins of ancient Rome.

WEIMAR. ILM PARK, TIEFURT, BELVEDERE

Around 1789, after a visit to Wörlitz, Goethe suggested creating an English garden in the valley of the Ilm. At Tiefurt, north of Weimar, Dowager Duchess Anna Amalia transformed her estate into an exceptionally beautiful (and well-preserved) landscape garden. In 1815 the gardens of the Belvedere Palace, south of Weimar, were also developed into a spacious landscape park.

SEIFERSDORFER TAL, NEAR DRESDEN

In 1781 Countess Tina and Count Moritz von Brühl began to transform a wooded river valley behind their residence into a dream landscape fraught with literary allusions. With a little imagination, one can still detect the spirit of sensitivity that pervaded this garden, which was a popular haunt in the eighteenth century.

MACHERN, NEAR LEIPZIG

In 1782 Heinrich August von Lindenau began to create an English garden at Machern. The high spot of its programme, which is dominated by Gothic and masonic motifs, is an imposing castle whose interior harbours many surprises.

LOUISENLUND, NEAR SCHLESWIG

This is a handsome landscape garden beside the river Schlei, though little has survived of its masonically-influenced building programme.

EMKENDORF, NEAR KIEL

An idealized landscape inspired by literature came into being at Emkendorf Manor, a meeting place favoured by artists and scholars, in the closing decades of the eighteenth century.

HAMBURG. ELBGÄRTEN

The bank of the Elbe between Altona and Blankenese was almost entirely remodelled in the English style after 1780.

MUNICH. ENGLISCHER GARTEN, NYMPHENBURG

In 1789 Elector Karl Theodor commissioned von Sckell to design the Englischer Garten, a public park in the English style. Between 1804 and 1823 von Sckell extended the Nymphenburg Palace's magnificent French park and, in an impressive manner, allied its Baroque symmetry with the laws and potentialities of landscape gardening.

KASSEL-WILHELMSHÖHE

At the end of the eighteenth century and the beginning of the nineteenth, one of Germany's most important landscape gardens was developed out of a Baroque mountain park. It still has some surprises in store, even today, including a huge Gothic castle (whose library formerly contained an extensive collection of thrillers).

BERLIN. TIERGARTEN, SCHLOSS CHARLOTTENBURG, PFAUENINSEL, GLIENICKER PARK

The Pfaueninsel [Peacock Island], with its small ruined castle and garden buildings, is still the 'purest' of Berlin's parks, whose history goes back to the eighteenth century. The Prussian Gardens were redesigned and enlarged during the nineteenth century, mainly by Peter Joseph Lenné. Charlottenburg's Baroque park, too, acquired areas of natural landscape. Glienicker Park, the loveliest of Berlin's landscape gardens, effects a smooth transition to the extensive gardens at Potsdam.

POTSDAM. NEUER GARTEN, SANSSOUCI, BABELSBERG

The uniquely coherent garden landscape in and around Potsdam is composed of numerous gardens and palatial buildings. This is where the Prussian response to the naturalism of the English garden took shape after 1800. The Neuer Garten, one of the most beautiful English gardens in Germany, was begun in 1786. Lenné also worked at Sanssouci, where he developed the idea of the landscape garden in his own way. Lenné's work on the spacious park of Babelsberg Castle was continued by Prince Hermann von Pückler-Muskau.

MUSKAU, NEAR COTTBUS

At Muskau between 1815 and 1845, Prince Hermann von Pückler-Muskau, who had travelled widely in England and particularly admired the work of Capability Brown (v. p. 103), devoted a great deal of effort and expense to creating a huge, idealized landscape. He thereby bequeathed posterity his own version of a romantic landscape garden, whose fundamentals he summarized in a book entitled *Andeutung über die Landschaftsgärterei* [An Outline of Landscape Gardening].

COTTBUS. BRANITZ

Having ruined himself financially by creating his huge park, the 'parkomaniac' (Pückler's own description of himself) moved to Branitz, where he created yet another nine-teenth-century masterpiece of garden design. Its highlight is the view it affords of a grassy pyramid set in a lake, the prince's burial place.

HOMBROICH ISLAND, NEAR DÜSSELDORF

During the 1980s a modern landscape park incorporating an historic garden was created on the island of Hombroich, south-west of Düsseldorf.

Bibliography

Sources

Where the origin of quotations is not apparent from their context, the literature on individual gardens will generally guide one to the relevant sources. For all that concerns Horace Walpole, see Norbert Miller's *Strawberry Hill. Horace Walpole und die Ästhetik der schönen Unregelmässigkeit,* Munich 1986; on William Kent, see John Dixon Hunt's *William Kent, Landscape Garden Designer,* London 1987; on Lancelot Brown, see Dorothy Stroud's *Capability Brown. An illustrated life of Lancelot Brown, 1716–1783,* Haverfordwest 1992. Other guides include Christopher Thacker's *The History of Gardens* and his compilation *England's Historic Gardens: An Illustrated Account of One Nation's Garden Heritage,* Dorking 1989.

On the individual gardens

Harris, John: *The Palladian Revival. Lord Burlington, His Villa and Garden at Chiswick,* New Haven/London 1994.

Hewlings, Richard: *Chiswick House and Gardens,* English Heritage 1989.

Woodbridge, Kenneth: *The Stourhead Landscape,* National Trust (London) 1995.

West Wykeham Park, National Trust (London) 1993.

Castle Howard, Birmingham 1988.

Fountains Abbey and Studley Royal, National Trust (London) 1993.

The History of Ripon, to which is added a description of Fountains Abbey, Studley, and Hackfall, York 1801.

The Rievaulx Terrace, North Yorkshire, National Trust (London) 1992.

Rodenhurst, Thomas: *Description of Hawkstone, the Seat of Sir Richard Hill,* 9th ed. London 1807.

Stowe Landscape Gardens, National Trust (London) 1997.

G. B. Clarke (ed.): *Descriptions of Lord Cobham's Gardens at Stowe (1700–1550),* Dorchester 1990.

Blenheim Palace, Norwich 1993.

Petworth House, West Sussex, National Trust (London) 1994.

Butlin, Martin; Luther, Mollie; Warrell, Ian: *Turner at Petworth. Painter & Patron,* The Tate Gallery, London 1989.

Further reading

Batey, Mavis; Lambert, David: *The English Garden Tour. A View into the Past,* London 1990.

Clifford, Derek: *A History of Garden Design,* London 1966.

Chambers, William: *A Dissertation on Oriental Gardening,* London 1772, reprint London 1972.

Everett, Nigel: *The Tory View of Landscape,* New Haven/London 1994.

Hobhouse, Penelope; Taylor Patrick (eds): *The Gardens of Europe,* New York 1990.

Hunt, John Dixon: *The Figure in the Landscape. Poetry, Painting, and Gardening during the Eighteenth Century,* Baltimore/London 1976.

Hunt, John Dixon: *Garden and Grove. The Italian Renaissance Garden in the English Imagination: 1600–1750,* London/Melbourne 1986.

Hussey, Christopher: *English Gardens and Landscapes. 1700–1750,* London 1867.

Jackson-Stops, Gervase: *An English Arcadia 1690–1990. Designs for Gardens and Garden Buildings in the Care of the National Trust,* Washington D.C. 1991.

Manwaring, Elizabeth W.: *Italian Landscape in Eighteenth Century England. A Study Chiefly in the Influence of Claude Lorrain and Salvator Rosa on English Taste 1700–1800,* London 1965.

Mason, William: *The English Garden. A Poem (1772–1781),* reprint New York/London 1982.

Mosser, Monique; Teyssot, Georges: *The Architecture of Western Gardens: A Design History from the Renaissance to the Present Day,* 1993.

Thacker, Christopher: *The Wildness Pleases. The Origins of Romanticism,* London 1983.

Turner, Roger: *Capability Brown and the Eighteenth-century Landscape,* London 1985.

Turner, Tom: *English Garden Design. History and Styles since 1650,* Woodbridge 1986.

Walpole, Horace: *The Castle of Otranto,* 1764.

All the gardens described in this book are open to the public. Those who wish to undertake an English garden tour will find all the information they need about the vast majority of important English gardens and country houses in one of the following two publications, which are updated annually: *Historic Houses, Castles and Gardens in Great Britain and Ireland*, East Grinstead, and *Visitor's Guide to Historic Houses and Castles*, London.

Illustrations

Endpaper (front and back): John Rocque, *Plan of Chiswick*, 1736 (photo: Geremy Butler); p. 3: *The Music Temple of West Wykeham*, painting by Thomas Daniell. c. 1790 (photo: Country Life); p. 4: Stowe, *The Temple of Concord and Victory* by J. C. Nattes, 1805 (photo: NTPL/Angelo Hornak); p. 11: from Christopher Thacker, *The History of Gardens*; p. 13: Kiel University, Kunsthistorisches Institut/University Library (photo: Carl Lamb); pp. 14, 124: from Dorothy Stroud, *Capability Brown*, London 1975; p. 17: The Egremont Collection, Petworth (photo: Mark Fiennes); pp. 20, 22: Geremy Butler; pp. 26, 31: from John Harris, *The Palladian Revival*, London 1994; p. 30: Chatsworth/Devonshire Collection; p. 37: Richard Bentley, engraving from *The Description...*, 1784; p. 40: Wilmarthen S. Lewis Collection, Farmington/Conn.; p. 42: from Laurence Fleming, Alan Gore, *The English Garden*, London 1979; pp. 50, 78, 84: NTPL/Angelo Hornak; pp. 55, 102: from Kenneth Woodbridge, *The Stourhead Landscape*, London 1982; p. 57: National Gallery, London; p. 58: from *West Wycombe Caves*; pp. 62, 63: Yale Center for British Art, Paul Mellon Collection; p. 68: from M. Batey/D. Lambert, *The English Garden Tour*, London 1990; pp. 72–3: David Lambert; p. 86: John Bethell; pp. 94, 96, 98, 100: Hawkstone Park Leisure; pp. 109–10, 112: Benton Seeley, 1750; p. 114: from Hammerschmidt/Wilke, *Die*